CUSTOM AUTO
Upholstery

How to design and create custom or repro interiors

Over 300 step-by-step photos and a gallery of examples

John Martin Lee

Motorbooks International
Publishers & Wholesalers Inc.
Osceola, Wisconsin 54020, USA   ®

First published in 1988 by Motorbooks International Publishers & Wholesalers Inc, PO Box 2, 729 Prospect Avenue, Osceola, WI 54020 USA

Motorbooks International is a certified trademark, registered with the United States Patent Office

Printed and bound in the United States of America

The information in this book is true and complete to the best of our knowledge. All recommendations are made without any guarantee on the part of the author or publisher, who also disclaim any liability incurred in connection with the use of this data or specific details

Library of Congress Cataloging-in-Publication Data
Lee, John Martin.
  Custom auto upholstery : how to design and create custom or repro interiors / John Martin Lee.
    p. cm.
  Includes index.
  ISBN 0-87938-323-2 (pbk.)
  1. Upholstery.   I. Title.
  TT198.L44   1988   88-19140
  747′.5—dc19   CIP

On the front cover: Beautiful upholstery is the finishing touch for a hot rod. *John Lee*
On the back cover: Two examples of integrated upholstery design. The custom upholsterer at work. *John Lee*

Motorbooks International books are also available at discounts in bulk quantity for industrial or sales-promotional use. For details write to Special Sales Manager at the Publisher's address

Thanks to all the people and firms who contributed to this book by furnishing information, catalogs, samples and photographs.

Special thanks to Norm Kyhn, Kyhn's Kustom Krafts, Longmont, Colo.; Ira Fazel, Mo Wilson and Curt Riley at Ira's Upholstering Service, Lincoln, Nebr.; and Larry McDaniel of Threadworks by Larry, Broomfield, Colo., who let me look over their shoulders, take pictures and ask questions about their work; and to Clyde Hill of Kirsch Fabrics, Omaha, Nebr. and Joel Oschner, Lincoln Auto Upholstery, Lincoln, Nebr., for technical assistance.

Contents

Introduction

In the past twenty-five years I have had the opportunity to photograph hundreds of customized cars and trucks. The results of these photographic efforts have turned up, at some point, on the pages of automotive hobby magazines. That kind of public recognition of their efforts and talents is one of the rewards these builders seek when they have spent months and years creating a car according to their concept of what a car should be.

In preparing a feature article for a magazine, I have the owner fill out a tech sheet noting all the modifications that have been made, brand names of

A dashboard padded and finished to match the other upholstery helps complete an interior theme.

This custom 1951 Mercury owned by Jack Walker is an exact copy of one built in 1952, right down to the dark green and white Naugahyde interior. The headliner has alternating white and green roll-and-pleat panels running lengthwise. Seats are of the classic horseshoe design, while stock trim divides the colors on the side panels. Kick panels and carpet inserts have a diamond pattern pressed in.

parts and components used, and giving credit to the individuals or shops that have performed various phases of the work.

These car owners often make their own living from one or more facets of the work, such as bodywork or engine building. Many times I'll find that an engine mechanic, for example, has also done his own bodywork and even painted the car himself. Or a bodyman has built his own engine and chassis in his spare time.

A lot of these tech sheets end up reading "all work by owner—except upholstery." The interior is the one phase of construction most often farmed out to a professional shop. If a wrench-turning mechanic could learn how to handle a spray gun well enough to shoot a good Candy Apple lacquer job on his or her street rod,

why, I often wondered, couldn't he or she learn to sew well enough to do the upholstery?

Maybe it goes back to the old sexual stereotypes: engine building and metal bending are masculine jobs, but upholstery involves fabric and sewing, and sewing is women's work. But if that's so, why have the most famous auto upholsterers—and many not-so-famous ones—always been men?

Certainly the special equipment necessary, or at least believed to be necessary, to upholster a car is a stumbling block. It's acceptable to buy a MIG welder to build your chassis and do bodywork, an engine stand to build the engine and a "cherry picker" to install it, but it's not acceptable to buy or rent a sewing machine to make seat covers. As we'll see later on, most of an upholstery job can be accomplished with no more than the tools found in an auto hobbyist's shop. A special sewing machine, while making the job quicker and easier, is a necessity for only a portion of the upholstering process.

Upholstery also seems to be the last and the least-planned operation of custom building a car. The owner delivers it to the upholstery shop only days before he needs it finished, and chances are he has given scarcely a thought to what he wants done on the inside. Instead of planning a theme and choosing fabrics and colors to go with it, he instructs the trimmer to "just do it like you did so-and-so's," or "I'll leave it up to you to come up with something."

What I hope to do with this book, then, is to take some of the mystery out of custom upholstery. It is a how-to book that will take you, step by step, through the commonly used techniques of upholstering and the tools involved. You will be given some direction on planning and designing your interior, steps to be mulled over in advance, just as you do in considering the car's drivetrain, styling and final color scheme. The upholstery may be the last operation undertaken, but it shouldn't be done as an afterthought.

If you choose, you should be able to follow the steps illustrated and upholster your car at home. Maybe you'll decide to do part of it and have the rest done professionally. Even if you decide not to tackle any of the upholstery job, at least you'll know what is involved—and why the trimmer you choose needs the time and money it's going to take. And, you'll have sufficient knowledge to discuss the job intelligently with the trimmer, direct him or her toward a favorite design, and choose colors and materials you'll be comfortable with for the next few thousand miles.

In the end, you may be able to save some money by doing your own work rather than paying a professional to do it, but best of all, you'll have the satisfaction of being involved in the process, not simply turning it over to someone else and hoping it turns out the way you want it to.

Chapter One

Auto interior design

My cousin and I have never kept in contact as closely as we should. Correspondence is usually limited to an exchange of Christmas cards.

His annual Yuletide note in 1968 mentioned that his current position in Detroit was with the styling department of Chrysler Corporation, and that he had worked on the 1968 Dodge Charger. I responded with congratulations on a beautiful job of styling the Charger; I liked it so well I'd bought one myself. He wrote back, "Thanks. I designed the bucket seats."

A well-thought-out, complete interior. Fine work such as this requires thorough plans, color and fabric coordination, and a bit of thinking ahead. In this Bel Air, the fuzzy dice complete the interior, matching the upholstery fabric.

That statement really made me realize how much the designing of a new car is a team effort, and what a small part any one individual has in that design. It's a long way from the image of a single artist laboring late at night over a drawing board, turning creative ideas into a complete new car design, outside, inside and underneath; many people and many minds are involved in creating a new car design.

In creating a custom car for your own use and enjoyment, you have an opportunity to be that individual at the drawing board. The car you create can be the culmination of ideas that are uniquely your own. Oh, it's not that the individual elements have never been used before; they have just never been assembled in the same way you have done.

No doubt you have given a great deal of thought to your custom car—the modifications you'll make to the body, the final paint job and wheel treatment, the ideal engine and drivetrain components. Have you given the same amount of thought to the interior?

Too often, it seems, this is a part of the design that is ignored or left to chance. In one instance I observed, the owner of a beautiful, new show car and several em-ployees of a trim shop were working frantically two days before a big show to finish the car's interior. Off to the side, the owner of the trim shop grumbled, "The bodyman has had the car for eighteen months. Now we're supposed to do the interior in a week!"

It did get done. The car owner was willing to pay extra for the whole trim shop crew to work overtime, including a Sunday and a holiday, to finish the job. And the car won top honors at the show. But this episode illustrates the degree of planning—or too often the lack of it—given to the interior of a custom project.

Types of vehicles

The kind of vehicle you're building or customizing will have an effect on the upholstery job you must plan for. It can be one of the determining factors in the choice of material and style, and it can have a definite influence on the cost and extent of work involved.

Street rods

The most widely acknowledged definition of a street rod is that of the National Street Rod Association (NSRA), which accepts street-driven vehicles

A modern street rod interior is likely to have body-supporting seats and conservative-colored fabric like the gray imitation mohair in Dave Tallant's street rod.

8

High-back bucket seats and consoles are at home in a street machine interior. The stereo and extra gauges are placed in a small, free-standing console in this 1955 Chevy. The gearshift lever is between the seats.

Vinyl materials and gimmicks like swiveling seats are more likely to be found in a custom car. The swing-out seats were introduced on Chrysler Corporation cars in 1959. Jerry Stanley rigged some up for his custom 1951 Vicky, which has nothing but period equipment and styling throughout.

originally manufactured, or of a body style that was originally manufactured, up through 1948. The vast majority of street rods use late-model engines and running gear. Because of the shortage of cars from that era, many street rods are built with fiberglass bodies that are replicas of the Ford and Chevy originals of the twenties and thirties.

Street machines

Street machines are a bit more difficult to categorize, but they are generally considered to be vehicles of post-1948 manufacture that have been modified for higher performance. This usually includes the use of later-model engines and running gear in earlier cars, and hopping up of the stock components on later models.

Street customs

The line between a street machine and a custom, or a street rod and a custom, is often fuzzy. Broadly speaking, custom builders emphasize body and interior work, and altering the appearance of the vehicle more than the performance aspects. The Kustom Kemps of America (KKOA), a national association of

Pickup owners often finish their stock bench seats with new upholstery covering, such as the tan velour that replaced the original vinyl in this late-model hauler.

9

custom enthusiasts, recognizes vehicles manufactured from 1935 through 1964 in its early, or leadsled, division. Those breaks overlap street rods and street machines, so it's up to the owner to decide whether his vehicle is a custom, rod or machine. Sometimes the particular event that is entered will be the determining factor.

Pickups

Pickup trucks usually fall into one or more of the previous categories, depending upon the year of manufacture and whether the emphasis is on styling or performance. There are also organizations and activities solely for pickups, especially street-driven early Ford and Chevrolet varieties. Many are also built for special purposes such as off-road rallying, pulling contests and mud racing.

Restorations

Returning an old car or truck to its original condition captures the fancy of more and more people all the time. Most want to recreate the car they owned or dreamed of in their youth, so the age of restored vehicles gets younger all the time. While this book deals with custom upholstery, the techniques are the same for duplicating a stock interior. You will be choosing

original materials or those closely matching the original, rather than special fabrics, and following the original style. In fact, you may have an advantage, because upholstery replacement kits are available for many models.

Special vehicles

There is a multitude of special-use vehicles, including racing cars, off-road race and rally machines, foreign sports cars and boats. Although some of these may have unique requirements for upholstery, the approaches and techniques discussed in this book should be adaptable to nearly all applications you may encounter.

Use of vehicle

How you plan to use your customized vehicle will play an important role in determining the upholstery job you plan and install.

A few cars are built strictly for the purpose of traveling to car shows—and winning awards! Owners transport them in enclosed trucks or trailers so they are not subjected to soil or damage on the highway. Engines are chromed and polished, and may not ever be started lest they get dirty or greasy.

Upholstery jobs in show cars are likely to be the fanciest you'll come across. The best of materials are

Although this Chevy Del Ray has been updated mechanically, owner Glenn George retained the stock interior and exterior appearance. The square-quilted panels are red vinyl, contrasted with flat panels in white.

used, and design and workmanship are impeccable. These jobs may include extensive extra work, such as upholstered panels in the engine compartment, underneath or on the running boards, which help the car garner extra show points. Show cars are a good place to get ideas and see the latest trends in styles and materials.

Probably most cars are customized with the intention of being driven on the street and entered in an occasional show. Some of them never get to the point of being show-worthy.

For a dual purpose like this, you have to strike a compromise, creating an interior that will be practical and wear well in daily use, but still be able to be cleaned up well enough for judging in a show. For instance, white, deep-pile carpet may look great under the lights at a show, but how well is it going to stand up to being walked on dozens of times between shows? A great set of seats with lots of heavily padded diamond tufts in black leather may not seem so great after you've sat on them for a thousand-mile trip during the dog days of summer. Are you going to open your trunk compartment to show judges and the public, or are you going to carry your luggage, tools and cleanup gear in it?

Of course, if you don't plan to show your car at all, but just use it for regular driving, your interior planning will lean more toward the practical. You'll want materials that provide the best combination of durability, comfort, easy cleaning and maintenance—with reasonable cost. Appearance will be mainly to please yourself and others who ride with you, not necessarily the show judge or the critical show patron.

Factory-original interiors are fine for vehicles in everyday use. Most of them, especially ones made of newer materials, can be maintained at a "show" appearance level with reasonable care. Auto manufacturers have spent millions of dollars researching ergonomics, or the relationship of the driver and passengers to the vehicle. A good place to start when planning your interior is to study new cars—how the seats are built, how controls are arranged, and the materials, styles and patterns employed. Then adopt or adapt these approaches for your own vehicle.

Special-use vehicles have different upholstery and interior requirements to consider. In a drag race car, for example, you may eliminate much of the upholstery to cut down on weight. The driver's seat needs to have safety built in but doesn't require as much comfort, since it's in use for only a few minutes at a time. An off-road racer also has to take safety and light weight into account, but comfort will be important to the driver spending hours behind the wheel bouncing over rocks, hills and deserts.

Vehicle styles

No doubt you have a particular look or style in mind as you set out to customize your car. Maybe it's

Intricate stitch work such as this is intended to win shows. This artistry is by Wayne DeCamp in his own full custom 1966 Thunderbird. The material is tan velour.

Black vinyl will wear well in regular use and still clean up to look good at a show. The smooth-grain black material in Jack Walker's custom Oldsmobile has a rectangular biscuit-tuft pattern with chrome buttons.

11

The plush padding and fabrics of a late-model luxury car appear in this contemporary interior. Dan and Sharon Botos transplanted dark brown velour power seats from a 1983 Lincoln Town Car into their 1957 Chevy.

Form-fitting, competition-style seats give a car a performance feel. These seats were specially built. Several designs are available from various suppliers in finished or unfinished form.

taking an ordinary street driver and making it look like an all-out race car. You may be bringing a twenty- or thirty-year-old model up to date with drivetrain components from a later model, and want to install a modern interior to match. Yet another approach is to customize a vehicle as it might have been customized during a particular period in the past.

What is in vogue in the late 1980s is the smooth look. The trend for street rods is toward plain, rather than louvered, hood panels, removal of extraneous trim and the integration of headlights, taillights and license plates into the body. Finishes are monochromatic, possibly with graphics, and much of the trim is either painted or polished aluminum.

Many street machines and a few customs are built with similar themes, utilizing painted bumpers and trim and solid colors for a clean, integrated look. Street machines are more likely to lean toward a performance appearance with hood scoops, front and rear spoilers, and race car–style wheels.

Custom cars are more likely to be designed to re-create the style of a particular period in the past. Since the heyday of radical custom bodywork was the fifties and into the first half of the sixties, most customs reflect this era. Some capture the styles of the hobby's infancy in the thirties and forties, and others, as mentioned, are done in a modern style.

A significant segment of the street rod population also adheres to period styles. These resto-rods are virtually restored to original appearance, with all accessories, but they employ modern running gear and interior components.

And, of course, you aren't likely to be happy for long with a stark, race car interior in a street-show car. Similarly, a candy-stripe interior design from the 1950s isn't going to look right in a contemporary-styled, "smoothie" street machine. Your upholstery style has to be coordinated with the overall style of the vehicle, in the same way the wheels, tires and other components are.

Contemporary interior styling seems to follow two main themes. One tends more toward comfort and employs soft padding and plush fabrics. Seats adjust forward and back, up and down electrically, and recline so the passenger can nap. Armrests and headrests are provided, and there's deep-pile carpeting underfoot.

The other theme leans in the direction of the enthusiast, or the performance driver, with more utilitarian finishes. Bucket seats are specially designed to wrap around the body and hold it securely during sharp cornering and quick acceleration.

Electronic equipment plays an important role in the contemporary interior. Dashboards and consoles are designed to accommodate computers, digital gauges and controls for exotic sound systems. Other portions of the interior are designed with stereo speakers, air conditioning outlets and even telephones in mind.

The factors to consider in planning your contemporary-style interior are whether it will be oriented for performance or comfort and what kind of equipment you need to plan for.

Certain interior styles are characteristic of particular periods in automotive history. The thirties, forties and early fifties were a conservative period in which interiors merely accommodated passengers. Bench seats were employed almost exclusively, front and rear, although the single-seat coupe and business coupe were popular. Rumble seats were still quite common until Ford's last one in 1939.

The less expensive models were upholstered with flat fabrics, usually in dull grays and tans with widespread use of pinstripes. Luxury cars were fitted with higher-quality fabrics and had overstuffed rolled and tufted padding. Leather was common in open cars and was also the preferred material for custom jobs of the period, both open and closed. Some use was also made in custom cars of friezes more commonly found on furniture.

The mid- and late-fifties brought on a revolution in automotive styling, color and power that also caught the interiors in its grip. While seating arrangements remained as they had been, flamboyant colors and designs of the exteriors were echoed inside. Vinyls that could duplicate the look of leather were widely used in both new and customized vehicles. It seemed an interior of Naugahyde or leatherette was a must in a custom or hot rod. Nylon and rayon ushered in a whole new world of durable, colorful and comfortable upholstery fabrics.

Changes in materials were more evolutionary than revolutionary during the sixties, but they were applied to some quite different interior designs. Influenced by the likes of the Chevrolet Super Sport, Chrysler 300, Pontiac Grand Prix and Ford Mustang, the bucket seat phenomenon was in full swing. The focus on performance mandated that a modified car have bucket seats and a floor-shifted transmission, and probably a center console, too.

The buckets-and-console trend continued into the seventies and branched out into several variations. Emphasis on safety brought headrests, first of all, and later the high-back seats with an integrated headrest.

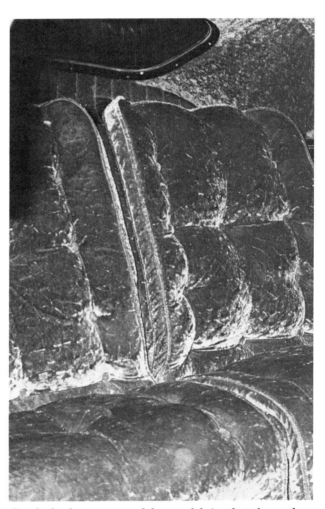

Nylon and vinyl made for more colorful and interesting interiors in the fifties. This pleated center section is a nylon brocade, surrounded by plain vinyl in a popular horseshoe design.

Crushed velvet was one of the new fabrics that changed upholstery styles in the seventies. The crushed finish is created by wadding up the material and squeezing it in a press when it is still hot from the manufacturing process.

13

Seats by Tea's Design are set into this street rod during the building process to determine fit in relation to other components. The seats, which come finished in a choice of wool, Dacron, vinyl or leather, will determine the choice of materials and styles for the rest of the interior.

This arrangement tends to put up a wall between front- and rear-seat passengers, which was further emphasized as opening rear-quarter windows on two-door cars were replaced with fixed "opera" windows. The rear seat became more of an enclosed, confined compartment.

Advancement in fabrics in the seventies created the nylon velvets and velours that came into wide popularity with both manufacturers and custom trim shops. Vinyls also advanced, with new perforated, breathable materials, making vinyl seating more comfortable. The popularity of leather was also revived, particularly for luxury models and for street rods which became increasingly sophisticated.

Scheduling the interior work

When in the building process should interior and upholstery work be done? There is no rule, but the important thing is to have this work scheduled along with the other work being done. You can't determine ahead of time the exact day or even the month, because there are too many variables that can force a change, but you can put the interior work into a sequence with the other tasks. That way it need not delay completion when everything else is done and you're eager to get behind the wheel. Planning ahead will also ensure that you have the necessary funds in your budget at the correct time.

Generally, interior work is left until the last, and for good reasons. The car is going to be surrounded by dirt, dust and grease as mechanical and bodywork proceed, and that's not a good environment for new upholstery. You're probably going to need access to the inside panels, floor, firewall and glass as you work, so the upholstered panels and seats will need to be removed anyhow. And you surely don't want the interior in place while you're painting doorjambs, window moldings and the dashboard. It's pretty hard to ensure that upholstery can be totally protected, even if only the exterior is being painted.

While you won't want to install new upholstery and leave it vulnerable to damage while you do the rest of your work, you can schedule the work at about any stage and then wrap the components in plastic or some other protective covering, and store them in a safe, dry place for installation when the rest of the car is completed. Upholstery work is something you can do in the house in the winter when you can't be in the garage wrenching on the engine or outside sanding on the body. It's also a task that can keep the project moving while you're waiting for parts or for a shop to complete some other operation.

Components and details

The principal reason for customizing a car or pickup is to personalize it, to make it a statement of the owner's character and his or her ideas of what a transportation vehicle should be. Auto manufacturers make machines for the masses. Individuals may choose to drive them the way they come, or change them to suit themselves.

The result of your customizing, it is expected, will represent for you an improvement in appearance, function, safety and comfort. Everything you do to your car, inside, outside and under the hood, should be considered against these criteria.

Chances are, you already have your project car and a plan for how it's to be customized. It will be built according to a certain style, with a particular favorite powertrain, and body modifications and a finish that will set it apart from the pack. Now it's time to design the interior—not after, but before, the rest of the package is done, or at least during the process.

Seats

The first element in interior design is where to sit and how to arrange the seating. The body style of the vehicle is the first determining factor to be considered. The single bench seat is the most basic, with the cushion extending the full width of the passenger compartment and accommodating two or three people. The single bench is found in coupes, roadsters, pickups, a few sports cars and some street machines in which the rear seat has been removed.

It may have a solid, one-piece backrest and even be incorporated into the passenger compartment, as in the case of early roadsters. Backrests that are split in the center to fold forward for access to the rear compartment are found most often in early coupes.

Later styles include the split bench, which has a cushion extending full width but divided into two sections that adjust individually, and the split back, which has an armrest that folds down in the center to divide the backrest.

Modern bucket seats originated in foreign sports cars and were so called because their shape resembled a milk pail with the sides cut away. They gave the driver a cushion that matched the shape of his or her posterior and a rounded backrest that wrapped partway around his or her torso to hold it erect and secure. The fascination with foreign sports cars after World War II led to the production of domestic varieties like the Corvette, Thunderbird, Nash-Healey and Kaiser Darrin in the 1950s. Hot-rodders and customizers began to pick up on the trend to sports car–style bucket seats, and manufacturers eventually responded. As production-line models such as the Chevy Super Sport, Pontiac Grand Prix and Chrysler 300 turned bucket seats into a trend, the seats became wider, better padded and covered in fancy leather and vinyl upholstery.

Now bucket seats show up in almost every type of vehicle. Most single- or one-passenger seats are called buckets, although the designs have gotten pretty far away from the original sports car variety. As a custom

Bucket seats originated in sports cars like this Corvette. The pleat pattern is heat-pressed into the vinyl material, a technique that allows manufacturers to offer a unique style for each individual model.

A solid bench seat used in a pickup, early coupe or roadster. Dale Boesch chose a black vinyl bench for his 1980 Forst pickup with wide, horizontal rolls and extra padding in the shoulder and leg support areas.

Modern-style bucket seats are often found in street rod coupes. In building these seats for Dave Tallant's 1933 Ford coupe, Bob Sipes built up bolsters with padding to support the passengers' sides and hips.

15

Individual bucket-style seats replace the bench in this pickup truck. Bob Nordberg had these installed in his late-model Chevy with a wide console between. The wooden top of the console has cutouts for beverage containers.

application, they are appropriate in street rods, customs, street machines and pickups.

Coupes, roadsters and pickups are restricted by space to a single bench seat or a pair of buckets. Most other cars likely to be customized are of the two-seat variety. They are club coupes (the short-top coupe body style with a rear seat, to accommodate four or five passengers), two-door and four-door sedans, two-door and four-door hardtops, convertibles and station wagons.

Two-door cars may have a bench seat in front with a split back to allow access to the rear, or a pair of front bucket seats. Either of these would be appropriate for a four-door car or station wagon, which can also use a solid-back front seat, since the back doors provide rear access.

The rear seat is usually a solid bench with a full-width, one-piece cushion and a solid backrest. When bucket seats arrived, many of the sportier interior designs began to incorporate padding and upholstery that sculpted the rear seat into a semblance of buckets to match the front. The Thunderbird rear seat, which curved around into the side panels, is still a popular starting place for some customizers. In the 1950s, Studebaker Starliner hardtops had a collapsible center armrest to divide the back seat for a sporty feeling.

At the extreme, there is also the four-passenger interior with bucket seats front and rear, and a center console running between them. Dodge's 1966 Charger had this arrangement and went a step further to have either of the rear bucket seat backs fold flat to extend the length of the cargo deck that was accessible through the fastback deck lid.

There have been various seating alternatives with station wagons. The most useful from a custom standpoint is the fold-down second seat that provides a longer cargo deck. A station wagon second seat might be a consideration for a custom application in a club coupe or sedan. It offers extra space for luggage, plus the option of seating for additional passengers as the need arises.

Those are the standard seating arrangements used in cars for the past few decades, and they aren't

A split-back bench seat is required for access to the back seat. The original one in this custom Mercury was brought up to date with mohair-like velour fabric.

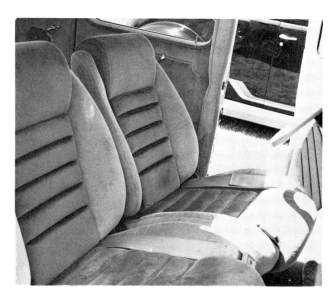

Front bucket seats offer comfort in this four-door street rod. Modern body-support styling and tan velour material similar to the original mohair are featured in this Model A.

The rear seat is usually a full-width bench as in this 1951 Ford Victoria customized by Jerry Stanley. White vinyl rolls and pleats are trimmed with burgundy piping that matches the exterior finish.

This custom interior has individual seats in the front and the rear. The seats were created by builder Ray Goulart who cut and reshaped them from the original bench seats. The full-length console was shaped from sheet metal, then padded with foam and covered in matching black vinyl.

likely to change drastically in the future. In designing a custom interior, however, you aren't bound by convention. You can feel free to experiment with other arrangements. Ideas can be drawn from van conversions. How about a rear-facing front passenger seat? Or one installed to swivel 360 degrees, coupled with a rear seat curving around the left wall of the passenger compartment to the back of the driver's bucket seat? It would give the car a sort of living room atmosphere.

Door panels

After the seats, the door panels probably get more attention than any other upholstered parts. Door panels hide numerous mechanical components while sealing out noise, dust, heat and cold. They are highly visi-

Ford's T-bird started the trend to rear seats wrapping around the corners. Jack DeJoy installed them in his 1949 Chevy custom with a combination of biscuit tufting on the lower portions and rolls and pleats on the top.

The second seat in a station wagon usually folds down for more cargo space. The owner of this Chevrolet Nomad chose vinyl for the second seat; vinyl offers both good wear properties and the correct period styling.

 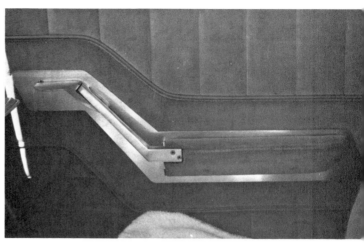

The design and material used on the door panel help to tie the interior together into a unified package. The same gray velour fabric is used throughout this Chevy street rod.

Door panel trim, whether early or modern, will help determine a panel's design, as the brushed-aluminum armrest from Valley Auto Accessories does in this 1934 Ford Victoria.

This 1956 Chevy business coupe came without a back seat. The owner upholstered the area in a velvet and vinyl combination to match the custom front buckets. Some custom builders remove the seat and finish the rear compartment the same way.

ble and can be an important component in tying the interior together into a package.

Door panels in older cars are most likely to be of upholstery board, a semirigid composition material cut to the shape of the door panel and flexible enough to conform to the gentle curve of many panels. The board is then finished with the upholstery material and attached to the inside door panel with clips or screws.

Door hardware such as handles, window cranks and armrests attach to the door's inner skin through holes in the upholstery board, and usually help hold the trim panel in place. Lighter hardware like electric window controls and decorative trim may attach directly to the upholstery board.

Cars built more recently may have complete door panels molded from some variety of plastic with armrests and hardware-mounting points molded in. Upholstery is then attached to fully cover the panel or to cover portions of it, creating a complete design in conjunction with the color and texture molded into the panel.

In customizing an older vehicle, you are most likely to be creating your door panel design out of fabric, attaching it to upholstery board and installing it on the door as a unit. The design possibilities are endless. They can range from a simple, one-color, flat covering to designs involving multiple colors and textures, and padded, three-dimensional designs of your own creation.

Quarter panels

The rear quarter panel covers the section between the door and the back seat in a two-door car and some early four-door cars on which the rear door doesn't extend as far back as the seat. It is also the side panel running from the seat to the rear door or tailgate on a station wagon or sedan delivery. Quarter panels, like doors, are usually made of upholstery board finished with fabric.

In interior design, the front door panels and rear quarter panels (and rear doors on a four-door car) should be considered as a unit. A design started on the front door panel may flow in through and continue or end on the quarter panel, or a design on the front door panel can be repeated on the rear quarter panel or the rear door. Whichever approach you take, make your design complete and compatible, as if the whole side were to be seen as one, uninterrupted by seats or doorposts.

Headliner

The headliner is the inside covering of the roof, from the windshield to the rear window and from one side window to the other. Headlining was once tacked to the wooden inner framework of early closed-body cars. Then for years, after solid steel tops became standard, the headliner was suspended from spring

The flat surface of a door panel lends itself to creative designs such as the geometric patterns stitched into the velour covering shown here. All the hardware has been eliminated from the panel by converting doors and windows to electric operation and locating the controls elsewhere.

steel rods that followed the top contour and attached at the sides. This is most likely to be the type of installation you'll be dealing with. More modern cars, actually from the sixties on, have often used a variety of foam, vinyl or fabric glued directly to the inside of the

In this car's interior, the theme of the front door panels is carried over to the rear quarter panels, and the rear seat is split in the middle to match the front. The same blue velour material and button design throughout serves to integrate the interior package further.

The headliner can be the focal point of an interior design. Here, a patterned velour is made up with pleats and buttons into parallel panels contrasting with the flat areas in an early sedan body.

roof or molded to fit the roof contours and held in place by various trim moldings.

The headliner is the ceiling of the car. As such, it is somewhat separated from the other interior elements and can provide contrast while still harmonizing with the rest of the theme. If the seats have rolls and pleats, for example, you wouldn't use a diamond button-tuft design on the headliner; a plain, single shade of one of the colors used in the rest of the interior will look just fine. The headliner is normally not as elaborate a design as other components.

The headliner can also become the focal point of your interior, since it offers the largest uninterrupted expanse of space. One builder, using fifties music as the theme for the interior, made his headliner in the design of the front of an old Wurlitzer jukebox with different colors of vinyl and even moving lights worked into the design.

Kick panels

These are the panels in front of the front doors, filling the space between the dashboard and the floor. They are usually made of upholstery board, covered with fabric and attached with screws or clips. They hide wires and cables and may contain outside air vents, air-conditioner outlets or stereo speakers.

Kick panels aren't something you want to draw attention to normally, so it's best if they're upholstered conservatively with a durable material. Use material that will carry forward the door panel design, or extend the carpeting from the floor up to cover the kick panels.

Package shelf

The package shelf, between the rear seat and the window, is a spot in the interior that's easy to overlook

A package shelf can be harmonized with the seats. Barb's Upholstery made up this cover in the author's former 1960

Pontiac custom with white, red and maroon vinyl matching the original-style seats.

but is still one that's readily visible, especially through the rear window. The way it's finished can have a strong impact on the overall effect of the interior. There was a fad in the late fifties and early sixties for covering the package shelf in alternating stripes of white and a color to harmonize or contrast with the car's body color, a bright scheme that reflected in the huge back windows of the day.

Package shelves are usually made of some sort of composition board finished to harmonize with the interior, but not usually upholstered, even in new cars. Covering the shelf is easy enough to do, however, and will give your car a completed appearance. Unless you're really after the fifties and sixties candy-stripe theme, plan to finish the package shelf with the material you're using for the seats, headliner or side panels. Short-pile carpet in a matching or harmonizing color will also blend well. You may want stereo speakers under the shelf or on the shelf, so plan that installation along with the upholstery work. Include the speaker grilles in your package shelf design, if they are to be exposed. You can cover over speakers with an open-weave material and it will not affect the sound, or you can perforate a material like vinyl or leather to allow the sound to come through while keeping the speakers hidden.

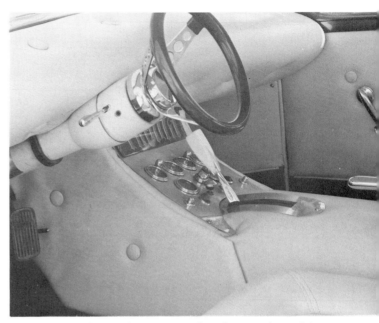

All gauges and controls were moved to the console on this radical custom built by Darryl Starbird. The original dash is covered with a heavily padded roll. The material is all—white vinyl with large buttons for decoration.

Dash and console

Dashboards have been padded and covered with vinyl or fabric going back at least as far as Chrysler's first postwar models which featured a crash pad to protect front-seat passengers in case of an accident. Since the dashboard is often the first area to deteriorate due to heat and sunlight, chances are you'll want to include a new covering in your interior design.

Here again is a small but important component of the interior. You may want to cover it to match the package shelf covering or to use the same material you're using on the seats and door panels. Since it's durable and attractive, there's nothing wrong with using vinyl on the dash, even if you aren't using it on other components—just be sure it harmonizes with the other colors. There's also nothing to prevent going wild on the dash, if that's in keeping with the rest of the interior. Remember, the dash is what you and your passengers are going to spend most of your time looking at, so make it something pleasing that will not be a hindrance by reflecting in the windshield.

Dash panels are usually made of steel, padded with fairly dense foam rubber glued to the surface, then finished with fabric stretched over and secured by glue or trim strips or a combination of the two. To get a good job, you may have to remove the dashboard.

The console came into use in the late fifties and early sixties, along with bucket seats. The sporty mode called for a pair of bucket seats with the console dividing them. At first it contained the gearshift lever and perhaps an ashtray and a small storage compart-

ment. Then tachometers, vacuum gauges, clocks and so on found a niche in the console, which now may hold drink trays, electric window controls and stereo receivers. It's like having an end table with all your little necessities beside your favorite living room chair.

If your car doesn't have a console and you're planning on using bucket seats, you may want to consider building one or taking one out of a junked car. It can play a major role in the interior design as the center for many of the controls. As for upholstery, consoles usually blend in with either the seats or the door panels.

You may install your stereo and accessory controls in a wood-grained or metal panel and not upholster the top of the console at all. If you do use upholstery on the top, since it is utilitarian, the best bet would be a vinyl that resists soiling. Carpeting generally extends up from the floor to cover the sides of the console.

Sun visor

Sun visors have been pretty much standard equipment for a long time. There was once a craze for finishing them in candy-stripe vinyl to match the rear package shelves, but unless you're going for that particular theme, it would be best to stay with the material you use for the headliner to make them blend in.

Some visors on new cars came with standard or optional vanity mirrors, which women, especially, appreciate for combing their hair or touching up

The armrest here is fitted with a pillow matching the seats. It is attached with buttons inserted through the door panel.

makeup. The visor is also a place to consider building in storage pockets for sunglasses, a pen, notepad and calculator.

Armrest

Armrests are often integrated with the door or quarter panel, and headrests with seats. These small items, however, may require special attention in the upholstery process. If you don't have headrests on your seats now, will you want to add them? Will they be built in or added on? If your armrests are now a separate part, attached to the door or quarter panel, you may wish to build them into your new panels. Center armrests, either permanently fixed or retractable, can be worked into front or rear seat designs, too.

Soft tops

Convertibles have a cover that snaps over the top well, hiding the folded convertible top. Being subjected to weather, soiling and abuse, these covers are usually made of vinyl but can be made up of other kinds of fabric. They continue the interior upholstery theme and serve as a bridge between the interior and exterior when the top is down. Here is a place to repeat a dominant interior pattern, such as a diamond or candy-stripe design. It can be a single thickness or padded and tufted, if desired.

Tonneau is the French term for the rear passenger compartment of an automobile. A tonneau cover is most often considered today as the fabric covering for a pickup bed. The sports car crowd in the fifties, however, used tonneau covers to protect their interiors while the vehicles were parked. They not only hid the folded convertible top, but extended over the front seat and steering wheel to the base of the windshield. You could often spot an MG or a Jaguar on the road with the tonneau over the passenger seat and top, but unzipped at the center to open the driver's seat.

Convertible and hot rod owners picked up the style for their cars, to protect the open passenger compartment from sun, dust or rain while the top was

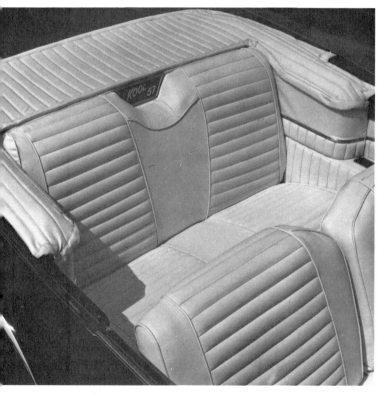

Top boots are often finished to match the upholstery. This 1957 Ford has one finished in white Naugahyde but with the roll-and-pleat pattern running perpendicular to that on the seats.

A tonneau cover protects a roadster seat from the elements. It's split in the middle to allow either just the passenger seat or both seats to be covered. To complement the car's early-style theme, this Model A also has a roll-and-pleat steering wheel cover.

down. Two-seat convertibles often had tonneau covers over the rear seat and top well. Some closed customs also had a tonneau fitted over the back seat.

The tonneau is basically an extension of the top well cover, so the same approach to upholstering it would apply. It can be flat or padded, plain or fancy, as long as it's in harmony with the interior upholstery. The larger area offers room for creativity in design.

Interior design considerations

I've talked quite a lot, up to this point, about various automotive seating and interior arrangements, types of vehicles and customizing styles and changes that have occurred in upholstery styles. Presumably, you by now have a general idea of the style of car you're aiming for and how you intend to use it when it's finished. Now it's time to actually get down to planning the interior for your car.

Color

One of your primary considerations will be color. Naturally, it should be something you like and will enjoy being surrounded by for the years you will own and drive the car. Assuming that the car will be driven reg-

ularly, it should also be comfortable. Black and dark colors tend to absorb heat, so dark upholstery will get hotter in the summer. Light colors, on the other hand, reflect the sun's rays and tend to be cooler.

The interior color must also coordinate with the exterior finish, which is one reason upholstery is usually the last step in building a car. Using the same principal color inside as you do on the outside is safe, but it may be too much of a good thing. Consider for the main part of your design scheme a contrasting color, with the exterior color for trim and highlighting.

Tan and gray go well with nearly any exterior color. That's why they're so commonly seen in street rods and street machines. These colors have taken the place of black and white, which were the colors of choice in the forties and fifties for the same reason: they went with everything. Red is a good color to contrast with black, white, silver or gray. Blue is also good with these colors. A yellow car can take many different colors for the interior—black, blue, red, green,

Neutral colors such as shades of gray—or tan and brown as on this Model A street rod door—are safe because they coordinate with many exterior colors.

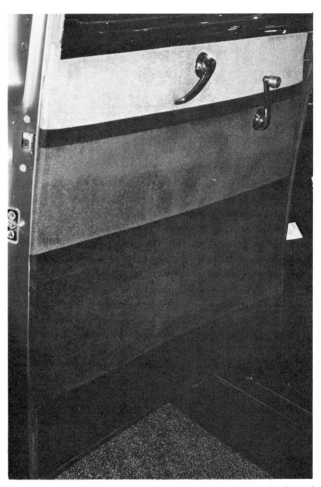

Four different colors—light gray, red and two shades of blue velour plus a bottom strip of dark blue carpeting—are combined in this 1940 Ford coupe interior. The exterior is also multi-hued.

23

Custom cars in the fifties often had vinyl roll-and-pleat jobs in alternating colors, known as candy stripes. A dark color, or one to match the car's exterior, alternates with white.

Button tufting in a diamond pattern can be in single or multiple colors. The off-white diamonds in this 1954 Ford convertible had to be individually sewn into the surrounding red crushed velvet.

brown. Lighter or darker shades of the exterior color are usually good, too, such as a light green interior in a dark green car, or dark blue upholstery in a light blue car.

The combinations are truly endless, and many unusual ones turn out to be quite pleasing. Tune yourself in to noticing different combinations of colors in nature, magazine ads, clothing and other objects around you.

One additional consideration is the color that is in the car already. If it will go with your exterior color choice, you may wish to plan the interior to take advantage of it. You'll get into quite a bit of extra work in refinishing the dash panel, steering wheel, window moldings and possibly other trim pieces to go with your upholstery.

Style

There seem to be no rules when it comes to custom interior designs, and that's good. It gives you free rein to do what pleases you. There are some things to keep in mind, however. Foremost is the style of the car. If you're building it to be an authentic depiction of a particular period in the past, you'll probably want your interior to reflect that, too. It's helpful to study styles that were popular during various periods.

Rolls and pleats

Basically, this is a design in which the material is formed into tubes that are filled with foam rubber or cotton to form rolls. The material is then tucked and sewn down between the rolls to form a channel, or pleat. This is also referred to as the tuck-and-roll style. It can be used for the entire design, or to make up various components such as inserts for bucket or bench seats and door and side panels.

The rolls can be of any size, from narrow, inch-wide ones that lend an intricate feeling, to heavily padded ones four or five inches wide which give an overstuffed look to an early-style street roadster or custom. Most rolls are done in intermediate, two- or three-inch widths. The width can vary within the design or stray from the usual straight-line format to create fan shapes, seashells, sun rays and other unique patterns.

Tufting

This style's appeal has always been the heavily padded, luxurious look. Originally, tufting was the practice of drawing together the cushion or object by passing a thread through at intervals and decorating the depressions so produced with buttons or tufts, a tuft looking similar to the flower of a dandelion. In common use today, tufting refers to the puffy surface created in the above manner, usually but not necessarily decorated with buttons.

Tufting is most commonly done in a diamond or square pattern, but many different shapes are possible. Elongated hexagonal shapes, or rolls ending in a half diamond highlighted with a button, are incorporated into some appealing designs. Here's a design element on which your imagination can roam freely.

Buttons

While most commonly associated with tufting, buttons are a decorative element in themselves. A fairly inexpensive upholstery job that relies on installing the material flat over a cushion or panel, without a stitched or padded design, becomes much fancier with the simple addition of buttons to break up the expanse. They can be formed into a design and pulled down into the padding to create the puffy look without the need for stitching.

Buttons are also useful in highlighting a tuck-and-roll job when used, for example, where vertical pleats intersect a horizontal roll. Where rolls and pleats may extend all the way across a seat cushion or back, a row of buttons can be used to divide the expanse into two smaller segments.

Buttons may vary in size from about 1/2 inch to 1 1/2 inches or larger, but 1/2 inch to one-inch sizes are preferable for most applications. They can be covered in any upholstery material, and you can decide whether you want them to match or contrast with your main upholstery color. In addition to the standard, round button, there are many possibilities for similar decorations in various shapes that have been applied on new cars in recent years. A trip through a salvage yard may net you a pocketful of upholstery ornaments to help make your interior unique.

Pillowback

A relatively new design concept, popularized by the new car manufacturers, is the pillowback. In this design, a separate piece much like a sofa pillow is at-

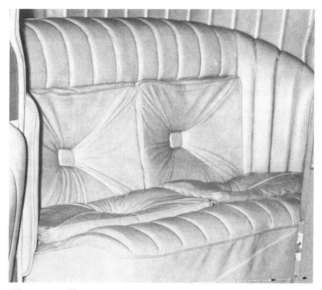

Buttons help decorate and give definition to a roll-and-pleat job. Plenty of extra padding is also incorporated to make the seats in this Chevy Nomad more comfortable.

Floating pillows attached to the seats lend a look of luxury to this street rod coupe. The pillows are highlighted with large, square buttons in the center.

tached to the cushion, to the back of the seat, or to both, making a pad to sit on. The pillow is softly padded and may be finished with buttons or loose pleats in the fabric. The pillowback style has a luxurious appearance and feel that makes it a natural for a custom or show car, but it is less appropriate for a performance-oriented machine.

Sculptured look

This style is also a modern phenomenon. Look for it to dominate custom auto interior styling for the next few years. Sculpturing yields the same plush, padded effect as tufting or tuck-and-roll styles, but in a slightly different manner.

Individual pieces are made up in a particular design, often following some other design element such as a door armrest, then filled with padding and attached to or inserted through an opening in the surrounding panel to create a three-dimensional effect. The sculptured elements are often done in another color or different texture of material to further emphasize the contrast.

Decorative stitching

Still another modern design component that will see greater play in coming years is decorative stitching. It has been used sparingly in the past but has tremendous potential for design creativity.

For decorative stitching, the surface material is placed over a thin (up to 1/2 inch) layer of foam padding, and then over a backing material, which may be a sturdy fabric for a seat or upholstery board for a door or side panel. A design is drawn onto the surface mate-

rial, then the piece is stitched on a sewing machine following the design. The design is permanently embossed in the panel, with the foam backing providing a sculptured, three-dimensional effect.

There are, of course, endless combinations of these design elements. Putting them together in new and creative ways is what can make your interior outstanding and uniquely your own.

Materials

I'll present a more complete discussion of upholstery fabrics in the next chapter. But as you plan and design the interior, you should keep in mind that certain materials are more appropriate than others for certain designs and themes. Leathers and vinyls seem to be appropriate for nearly any situation and style, and they have been used in new cars continuously since the fifties.

Practically all custom and street rod interiors in the fifties were vinyl or leather, so those are safest if you're strong on authenticity. Some of the newer perforated and breathable vinyls are more comfortable and decorative but still retain most of the authenticity. They have a great deal of potential for a wide variety of future uses.

The newer fabrics such as velours and velvets are attractive, comfortable and easy to work with. They have gained universal acceptance in modern street rods and are also gaining wider use in fifties-style cus-

Unique designs are created with sculptured upholstery styling. Bob Sipes created this styling in Roger Ward's 1953 Chevy sedan delivery in tan vinyl. Tiny holes perforating the material used on the inserts give it a different texture, creating contrast.

Wayne DeCamp created intricate, stitched designs in the underhood cover of his custom Thunderbird.

toms with either traditional or modern designs. Any of these are also applicable to street machines and trucks. Vinyls continue to be more appropriate and practical for special uses such as racing and off-road driving.

Begin with photos

By now you should have a pretty good idea of what you want for your interior—the color, style and generally the type of material. Now it's time to sit down and seriously design your interior. This step is sort of like making a blueprint to give you a fairly accurate idea of what the finished product will look like and to provide directions to follow in assembling it.

Photographs are probably the best place to start. Begin by photographing the car you're going to be working on. Use a fast black-and-white film like Kodak Tri-X. Turn the car directly *away* from the sun. This will minimize the contrast between bright spots and shadows, and give you clearer pictures. Expose for the amount of light on the portion of the interior you're shooting, then use a flash to light it better and fill in the shadows.

Photograph the interior as a whole as completely as possible. Use a wide-angle lens, if available. Photo-

graph it from every angle, then shoot the individual components in detail. Have the black-and-white film developed and printed; the shots you choose to work with can then be enlarged into 5 × 7 or 8 × 10 prints. You can take these prints to a copy shop to have the size enlarged or reduced. Make several enlarged photocopies of your photos. Being on paper rather than as photographic prints, these pictures will be easier to draw on, color and cut-and-paste.

You can also collect other photos to help you. Take the camera to car shows and photograph the interiors and components you may want to incorporate into your design. Don't be afraid to go to a new-car showroom or dealer's lot and (with permission, of course) photograph some interior designs you like. This is also where you can get a "feel" for some of the materials manufacturers use—as long as your hands are clean. Still another source of ideas is a furniture store. Many furniture fabrics and patterns aren't appropriate for auto upholstery, but you can see, and picture, a wide variety of colors and designs.

Study the hobby magazines that deal with the type of car you're going to upholster. This is the best source for determining what's current in interior styling. *Car Craft, Hot Rod* and *Popular Hot Rodding* are

The velour style of the seventies and the vinyl style of the fifties are combined successfully in this 1948 Ford convert- *ible. The seats have roll-and-pleat inserts of velour surrounded by vinyl, both in shades of tan.*

some of the readily available titles that show trends in street machines. The street rod, custom and custom pickup segments of the hobby are covered by *Street Rodder, Rod Action* and *Truckin'* magazines.

New model brochures are also a source of interior ideas. They are in color and show you color combinations available from the factory. These can help you with your color scheme. If you should be lucky enough to find a factory brochure on your particular car at a swap meet, it may have the interior pictures you need, and you can skip the whole photographic step.

Armed with all these pictures and brochures, take some time to sit down with paper, pencil and eraser, and sketch out your own interior or trace it from a photo or brochure. You can use colored pencils or markers to try out colors and combinations on your drawings. It may even be advantageous to cut colored pieces out of the brochures and trim them to the size of your interior components, then stick them onto your sketch with rubber cement to see how the color looks.

This is the time to work on your "blueprint." Determine how a particular pattern is going to flow from one area to another, or how a design element will be applied to various components.

You can even make your plans to scale. Say, for example, an actual seat measures fifty inches wide. You make your sketch or print of the seat ten inches wide (the reducing/enlarging copy machines can be a big help). The scale is 1:5; one inch on the sketch equals five inches on the seat. If you want to see how $2\frac{1}{2}$ inch wide rolls and pleats will look, draw the lines to indicate the pleats, or channels, every $\frac{1}{2}$ inch on the sketch.

In this scale, one-inch or two-inch spacing would be a little harder to figure, but you can estimate and come out pretty close. For example, $\frac{5}{16}$ inch plus $\frac{5}{16}$ inch plus $\frac{5}{16}$ inch equals $\frac{15}{16}$ inch, or just about one inch, so slightly over $\frac{5}{16}$ inch is the measurement for two-inch rolls. As you'll learn to do when you actually work on the upholstery, begin at the center and work toward the outside in either direction.

These same techniques can be applied to other components of the interior. In laying them out on paper, be sure to account for the location of handles, armrests and other hardware.

Car shows are a good place to see and photograph a variety of interior ideas.

The rumble seat and front seat harmonize in this 1934 Ford roadster owned by Alan Egelseer. Burgundy leather was formed into two-inch rolls and pleats for the center sections and surrounded by a horseshoe. White piping separates the sections.

Gene Paist sewed the vinyl coverings for his 1937 Buick coupe in alternating rolls of yellow and white to go with the yellow exterior. At four inches, the rolls are wider than usual for candy stripes.

A Model T touring body has wide, four-inch rolls on the seats and extra padding to form fuller rolls around the back, sides and front. The fiberglass body has no doors, so the upholstered outer rolls are continuous. The material is a smooth-finish brown vinyl.

Jack DeJoy installed Thunderbird front buckets, as well as the wraparound rear seats in his 1950 Chevy custom. The camel-color velour is formed into rectangular tufts on the bottom, and vertical rolls and pleats on the top with a band of dark vinyl separating the sections.

Cloth woven with a two-tone chain-link design covers wide rolls on the seat and door panel inserts of this street rod, and heavily padded rolls of a solid color form the edges. A fold-down center armrest has been adapted from a later-model car.

Dark-blue flat cloth wraps around the corners of the cockpit of Mike Welch's Model A roadster, while panels of light blue, white and red stripes form a sort of racing design. The custom-built seat has a fold-down armrest.

30

The black interior of two-inch rolls and pleats in Bob Oman's black 1950 Mercury is very tasteful. The pleat pattern carries all the way across the seats from top to bottom but is outlined by stock chrome trim on the doors. Vertical pleats also cover the lower seat framework.

The two-inch roll-and-pleat pattern in this 1957 Ford convertible runs across the seats but up and down on the side panels. The color is off-white throughout to contrast with the red exterior.

The Detroit designers, maybe taking cues from custom builders, put some beautiful interiors into production cars

during the 1960s. This is a 1964 Galaxie 500 XL with roll-and-pleat vinyl in two-tone turquoise.

Larry Purcell used the traditional horseshoe design for his custom 1941 Ford coupe. Pleats run all the way across on the cushion but form individual back positions.

Car bodies were enclosed in the teens and twenties, and new cloth fabrics were developed, but button tufting remained a common motif. This one has half diamonds in conjunction with channels and wide rolls.

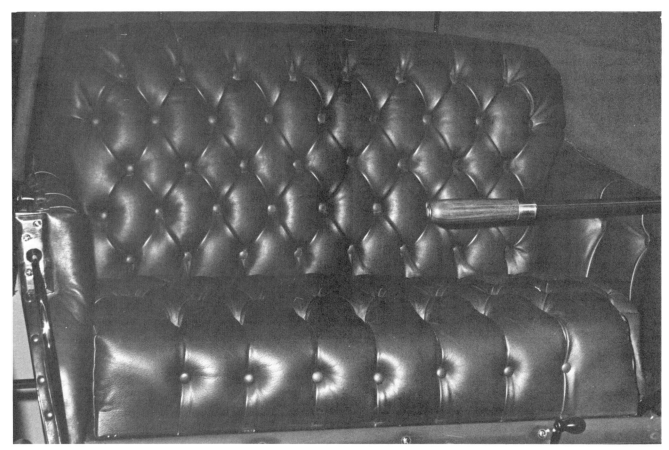

Most of the early "horseless carriages," like this tiller-steering model, had button-tufted leather seats. The width of the diamonds should be between one-third and two-thirds of the height.

A Thunderbird rear seat was cut down to fit the back of this 1960 Impala convertible. The split cushion and pillow-type back goes well with the individual front seats. The upholstery material is a dark-blue napped fabric like that commonly found in contemporary luxury cars.

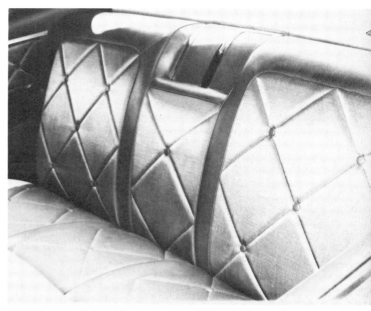

A bold diamond pattern is topstitched into a nylon cloth cover material and set off with buttons at the intersecting points. Inserts are trimmed with a contrasting vinyl.

High-back bucket seats finished in red velour and vinyl make traveling comfortable in Jim Welty's 1934 Ford. Seat bases are made from wood and incorporate beverage holders in front.

The imagination is the only limit in custom interior designing. The theme Bob Sipes created for Ed Guffey's custom Ford symbolizes a flower in white opening out of a blue stem, all stitched in vinyl over custom-built seats.

Wayne Kemp accomplished a candy-stripe variation with two shades of red alternating in the roll-and-pleat panels of his 1964 Impala. The solid panels are of the lighter shade and piping is white.

Form-fitting Mazda RX-7 bucket seats flank a Corvette console in Roger Ward's 1954 Chevy. Although the fawn color is the same, contrast is provided by perforated vinyl for the inserts against smooth vinyl borders.

For Dennis McClure's 1948 Ford convertible, Ron Nelson covered Datsun 510 bucket front and bench rear seats in

dark gray leather. The tuft design is accomplished by pulling the cover into tucks, but without buttons.

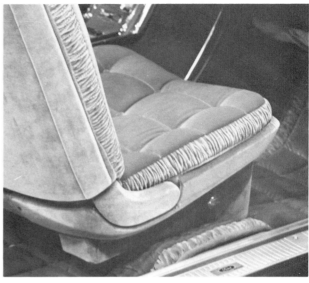

This thickly padded seat from the forties takes on new character with a stitched vinyl center design in velvet inserts, surrounded by a vinyl border.

The velour material decorating the edge of this Thunderbird seat has been "gathered," which means that small tucks are taken in the material and held while the edges are sewn to permanently secure the wrinkles.

Red crushed velvet matching the interior lines this 1947 Chevrolet trunk. Panel board is covered for the back and sides, and the material is glued directly to the wheelwells. The upholstered box hides the trunk-mounted battery.

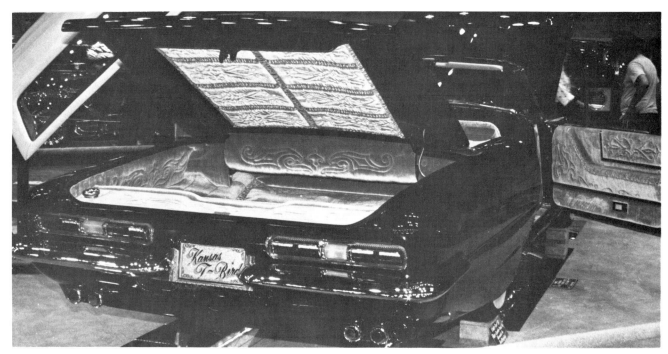

*Wayne DeCamp went all-out in upholstering his 1966
Thunderbird. Stitched velour panels fully line the trunk.*

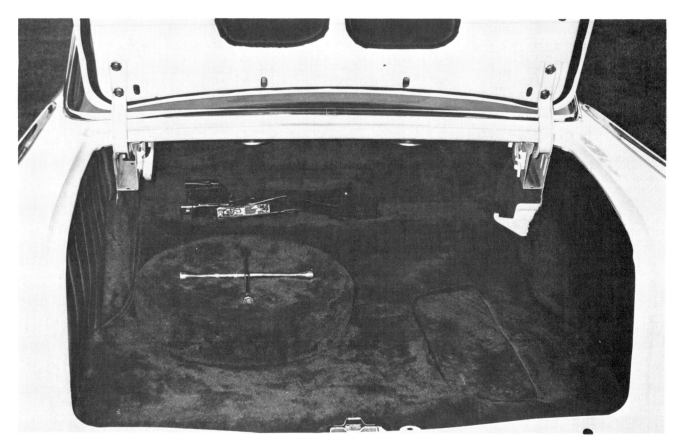

*This 1957 Chevy trunk is neatly decked out in dark brown,
short-nap, cut-pile carpet—including a tire cover. The
former tire well is now a hidden storage compartment. The
side panels are covered with matching pleated velour.*

For his radical custom 1951 Mercury, Dave Stuckey rebuilt the dashboard, putting all instruments into a pod jutting out at an angle to the driver's right. The entire dash panel is padded and covered in grained vinyl.

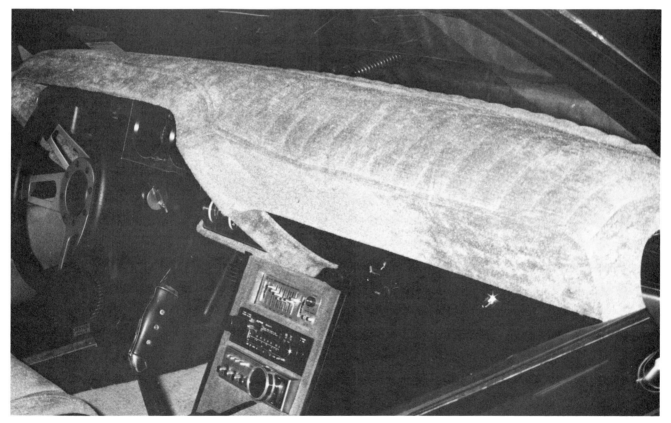

The vinyl dashboards in late-model cars have a bad habit of cracking. This owner has covered his with velour matching the seats.

Going a step further than merely carpeting the rear cargo deck, this Chevy Nomad owner added button-tufted velour inserts on the floor and on panels built to finish off the back side of the rear seat. The rear seat has also been split into two buckets with a console between like the front.

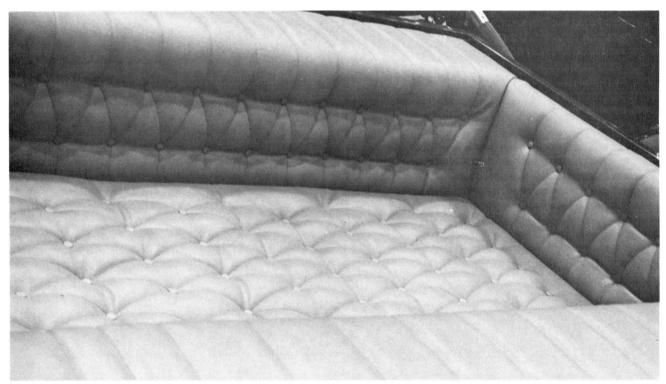

To deck out a pickup truck for show, this owner cut panels and built boxes to run along the sides, then covered all with thickly padded, button-tufted vinyl. The pattern is diamond on the floor and half diamond on the sides.

Steering wheel covers were once the rage, along with rolled and pleated rear cargo deck and sun visor covers. Norm Kyhn sewed this wheel cover out of Naugahyde to give his 1947 Plymouth coupe a fifties look.

Overhead consoles provide additional space for extra instruments, switches or reading lamps. The one in this 1967 Mustang is finished in brown, grained vinyl, as are the windshield posts, dashboard and header panel.

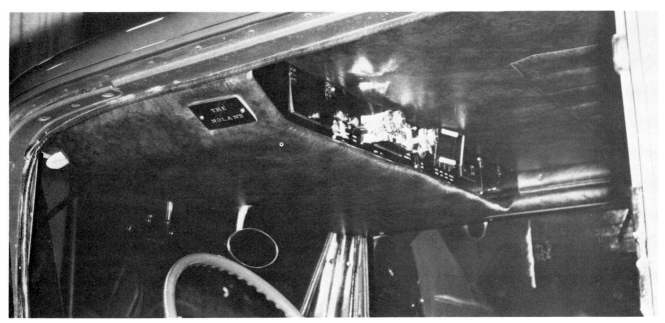

The overhead console in John Nolan's Chevy street rod contains the stereo, CB radio and storage compartments. It is finished like the headliner, in vinyl.

While most street rod builders replace the rubberized top inserts in old car bodies with metal, this owner took advantage of the opportunity to show it off with a deeply tufted vinyl insert.

This street rod owner had the brand name stitched into the vinyl cover for the side-mount spare tire. Virtually any design can be duplicated with stitching.

Chapter Two

Upholstery fabrics

Whenever Detroit's auto designers and engineers approach production stage in the development of a new model, outside suppliers are given specifications for the many materials and components necessary to build the vehicle. From these specifications, suppliers prepare their proposals to provide a quantity of a certain product at a specific price.

Among the corps of suppliers are textile manufacturers, whose basic specifications for interior materials cover such characteristics as weave, fiber content,

Many vinyl grain patterns and colors are continuously available, making it possible to match the most common ones used in past years.

finish, weight, strength and colorfastness. Textile industry representatives then set up showings of the fabrics in their line for the interior styling section. The stylists may consider thousands of samples before selecting a few they feel are appropriate to their project. The companies then furnish enough material to hand-trim prototype bodies of the new model, which are presented to the engineering and sales departments for their input into the final decision on the fabrics to be used.

The fabrics are also tested by machines that inflict as much wear in an hour as the material would get in a year in the car. Other machines demonstrate the effects of rubbing against typical suit and dress fabrics. Further tests determine the tearing point of the fabric, its thread count and how much or how little it stretches. The results are compared to the standards set by the trim department.

With approval of the models and successful passage of the quality tests, the fabrics are ordered by the manufacturers in quantities sufficient to cover their projected production of that model.

A special fabric design such as this pattern woven in several shades of brown and tan will probably be discontinued soon after a manufacturer is through using it. The best plan is to buy all you're going to need at one time.

Thus, the automobile industry together with the textile industry determine what the interiors of new cars will look and feel like. Certain materials that serve well and meet consumer acceptance may be continued for several years. Some popular fabrics and vinyls are continued, with variations in the styles into which they are finished.

Especially distinctive designs, such as the denim blue-jean and woven Indian-blanket styles introduced by American Motors in the 1970s, may have a life span of only a year or two in one specific car model. Once that model is discontinued, it will probably be dropped. That's why it can be impossible to obtain an exact match of the original material when restoring a car. Sometimes the demand for some materials, such as the pressed waffle-pattern vinyl in some 1955–57 Chevys and the unique woven tweed cloth of 1956–58 Plymouth Furys, becomes sufficient to warrant remanufacturing it for the restoration trade.

A few colors and designs stay around because car makers continue to order them, or because they are in sufficient demand in the aftermarket or retrimming trade. There are several more or less standard vinyl grain patterns, while others may come and go. Certain napped fabrics of the velvet-velour-mohair line or single-color flat weaves may continue in demand, while others may not be available a year or two from when they were first produced. The lesson here is, if you upholster your seats now, don't take it for granted you will be able to get matching material for the door and side panels three years down the road.

Manufacturers call the shots on interior materials by what they offer to the public. They own the patterns. When the mill fills an order for a manufacturer, there's usually an overrun, which the mill retains. After the model for which it was produced is discontinued, the auto maker will release the surplus. The mill can then sell it to jobbers. That usually takes place about the time a new model is introduced. In other words, when production of the 1989 model begins, the 1988 fabrics are released. If the particular model has met with poor sales, the manufacturer may also have a leftover quantity of the fabric to offer the jobbers.

Auto upholstery fabric suppliers are able to buy their goods inexpensively at that time, but they usually have to "sit on it" for some time. Demand from trimmers for replacement material doesn't get strong until the model is at least five years old.

Distributors stock or can get most materials that have appeared in new cars for the past ten years or so. If you like a weave, color or pattern from a fairly recent model, chances are pretty good you'll be able to get it unless the model was very unusual and produced in extremely low quantities. The most available fabric would be one offered in several of the manufacturer's models, because the distributors know there will be a demand and will have stockpiled it.

Sometimes the textile mills will, on their own, make up quantities of a particular fabric that is quite similar to the product made for the auto industry. This is then offered to the aftermarket or retrimming trade.

Besides being available, a fabric from a late-model production car is a good choice because you're assured it is suitable for automotive application. Some fabrics may be fine for furniture but will not perform at all well in an automobile.

It never hurts to find out how well a material performs in its original setting. If you have a chance, study the five-to-ten-year-old cars on a sales lot or in a salvage yard to see how their upholstery has held up. Has it become worn, split or frayed from passengers sliding in and out? Is it weak and brittle from the sun, or unusually faded? Has it become soiled or stained by perspiration, food or moisture? Check the interiors of cars at a custom car show, too, to get an idea of which materials seem to retain their appearance the best. Such observation will help you make an intelligent choice of material for your project.

Fabric history

In the beginning, there was leather. Leather was used to upholster the seats of buggies, carriages and wagons. The first automobiles were little more than buggies with motors, so construction techniques and materials, including upholstery, carried over from the old to the new. Inasmuch as early cars were all open to the elements, offering at best a folding top, the use of water-absorbing natural fabrics would not have made much sense. Leather, on the other hand, was tough and repelled water to a degree.

Leather is the one material to survive through the years. It still has widespread application today for upholstering upscale automobile models. Like everything else, it has changed and is now better and more versatile than the leather produced around the turn of the century. Its properties and applications will be discussed in greater depth later.

Closed cars came along later and, eventually, so did other types of upholstery materials. Initially they

Naugahyde or leatherette was the leading material for custom interiors in the fifties. It was developed as a less costly alternative to leather.

were adapted from the fabrics found in furniture upholstery. Later, new fabrics using synthetic fibers were developed especially for automotive upholstery applications. These fabrics have almost entirely replaced the natural fiber fabrics, except in cases in which the precise original fabric is specified for an authentic restoration.

To clarify terminology at this point, "fabric" refers to a cloth made by weaving, knitting or felting fibers. "Textile" is another name for fabric. The threads or filaments that are woven to make fabric are fibers, which may be either natural or synthetic. Real leather is a natural material made by tanning animal hides. Since it is not woven, leather is not a fabric. Vinyl, a material constructed of a polyvinyl plastic coating bonded to a woven or knitted backing, is considered a fabric. I will use the terms fabric, cloth, textile and cover material interchangeably in this book.

Fabrics may be woven flat, as an ordinary shirt would be, or with a nap, with upright threads giving the material a fuzzy look and feel. The nap is also known as the pile.

It is important to remember, when planning upholstery and shopping for materials, that the fiber in the weave (for example, nylon, polyester or wool) has certain characteristics that determine durability, colorfastness and feel. How the fibers are woven determines the type of fabric, such as velvet or flat cloth.

Woven fabrics were used almost universally in closed cars from the 1920s to the 1950s, when the plastic or vinyl materials came into widespread use. Cloth has come back strong in the 1970s and 1980s for standard and upscale new car models, with vinyl more common on economy models. Whereas the prewar fabrics were mostly natural fibers, fabrics today are primarily synthetic.

Custom upholstery trends have followed those of the new car industry. From the late 1940s into the 1960s, you had to have leather, Naugahyde or leatherette to have a true custom interior. Although leather and vinyl remain very popular, the trend during the 1970s and 1980s has been toward cloth; colors are conservative compared with the wild combinations of earlier years.

Fiber types

Many of the upholstery fabrics you'll have to choose from will be blends of two or more fibers—synthetic, natural or a combination of both. Different fiber characteristics make them more or less suitable for automotive upholstery applications and may affect where they're used in your interior. A popular fabric for couches and chairs, for example, may be totally unsatisfactory for auto seat covers because it won't stand up to constant exposure to the sun's rays or to the type of wear caused by passengers sliding in and out. Many do-it-yourselfers have made the mistake of using an unsuitable furniture upholstery fabric in their cars.

The following discussion should help you avoid that kind of mistake.

Natural fibers

Natural fibers are those derived from plants or animals. Wool and cotton are the most common ones found in auto upholstery fabrics. Linen and silk are others that may appear in furniture upholstery. Jute has been employed as backing for carpeting, and burlap, produced from jute, is an inexpensive material for covering springs.

Cotton

Cotton is the most common natural fiber to be found in upholstery today, and even it is not common. It is most widely used as a blending fiber, usually with polyester. The resulting fabric is superior to pure cotton in most respects.

Cotton's advantages are its ability to retain color and the cool feel that results from its natural ability to pass air through the weave, or breathe. On the other hand, cotton does not wear particularly well, and it is easily stained and difficult to clean, although application of surface treatments (such as Dow Gard or Scotch Gard) improve both its soil resistance and wearability.

Wool

The only other natural fiber found in auto upholstery cover material is wool. It wears very well. Some consider its natural look, which is quite dull, and its somewhat harsh feel, advantages, while others find these characteristics are undesirable. Since the fiber allows air passage, wool is quite comfortable to sit on for extended periods. High cost is the main strike against it.

Wool is offered as an optional covering by manufacturers of custom-built seats, and the yardage is available in several colors for custom upholstering. Wool is pliable and easy to work with. Restorers use wool to retain authenticity in a restoration, and it is the principal fiber in genuine mohair. Some owners also prefer wool for their carpeting.

Synthetic fibers

The revolution in the textile industry began in 1935 with the introduction of nylon by DuPont. Much stronger than any of the natural fibers then in use, the new synthetic was inexpensive to make and could be dyed any color. During the 1950s it was combined with cotton and acetate, another synthetic, for an upholstery cloth better and cheaper than pure nylon. Nylon thread eventually replaced weaker cotton thread for stitching.

The synthetics development started by nylon also produced other fibers with characteristics that make them even more appropriate for auto upholstery. Polyesters like DuPont's Dacron now make up much of the upholstery material on the market. Although rayon's ability to take and hold brilliant color has made it useful in blends with high color contrast, other characteristics make it less suitable as an auto upholstery fabric. More and more acrylic is appearing in US mills as they become more comfortable working with this European-developed synthetic.

Synthetics are manufactured in one of two processes. Nylon, polyester and acrylic come from the process of polymerization, while rayon and acetate are cellulose based.

Most of the upholstery material to be found today is synthetic. It may be all of one fiber, a blend of two or more synthetics or a synthetic blended with a natural fiber. Often the fabric's nap will be of one fiber and the backing of another. Synthetics dominate because they are relatively inexpensive, exhibit superior strength and long wear, are not subject to bacterial attack and organic decay and can be produced to closely duplicate the desirable properties of the natural materials.

Nylon

The most common of the synthetics, nylon can be produced in a wide variety of forms for different end uses. Being very strong, it can be made in very fine filaments and woven into a fabric that will be very light and flexible but still capable of long life. Nylon is also the only fiber that recovers totally to its original shape after stretching. It can be woven with a smooth or a harsh feel, can be dyed any color and can be given a shiny or dull finish. It does, however, retain a sheen that sets it apart from the natural look of cotton or wool.

Nylon's lack of absorbency can be both a help and a hindrance; it is easily cleaned and dries quickly, but it tends to feel clammy and uncomfortable next to the skin, especially for long periods in hot weather. Nylon won't burn, but will melt if it comes into contact with a flame or spark. It also tends to tear easily, yielding even to coat zippers and other dull objects. It is not the best material for color retention, tending to yellow or fade on the surface with prolonged exposure to sunlight.

Thanks to its versatility, nylon is found in all types of interior fabrics—velvet and velour, flat cloth, headliner material and carpeting.

Polyester

Dacron, a product and trade name of DuPont, is the most prevalent of the polyester fibers. It is close to nylon in strength and resistance to wear, although it

Most of the modern napped fabrics are nylon or Dacron, but they are made to look and feel like the wool mohair found in cars decades ago.

Nylon has a characteristic sheen and excellent wear properties. It will be found in the seat and panel cover fabric as well as the carpeting.

Velvet with nylon or polyester pile, as seen on the lower portion of this custom Mercury door panel, is common in new cars and as a retrimming material.

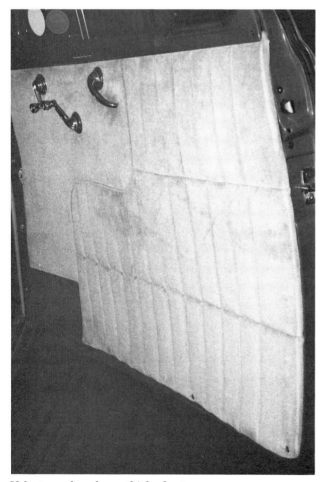

Velvet or velour has a thick, short nap.

will not stand up as well to extensive weaving. It takes and retains color well and can produce a range of textures from very soft to harsh. Its appearance can range from glossy to dull.

Velvet with a polyester pile is the number one fabric in current Detroit offerings. Polyester may appear alone or blended with cotton and is also common as the woven backing for pile fabrics and vinyls.

Acrylic

What nylon has been to the US textile industry, acrylic has been to the European industry—the top-selling upholstery fiber. With most major US mills making it now, and selling it for the same price as most nylon and polyester, acrylic is making great gains in application. Acrylic has superior ability to hold both color and strength when exposed to ultraviolet rays. It is on a par with nylon in wear and durability.

Like nylon, acrylic has a smooth, soft feel. Unlike nylon, it has a somewhat dull finish, which can give it the look of wool at a greatly reduced cost. It is most often woven as a pile fabric, or as the surface fabric in a pile weave, and is good for general interior applications.

Rayon

The ability of rayon to take and retain bright colors is offset by its relatively poor performance in strength and durability. Rayon is not found very often in automotive upholstery fabrics except possibly as a blending fiber in fabrics with high color contrast.

Polypropylene

Two of the better-known brand names of this synthetic are Herculon and Olefin. Having very low resistance to the effects of ultraviolet rays on both fiber strength and colorfastness, these fibers are not suitable for any extensive automotive use. Less expensive than some others, these fibers may appear in blends with other, more-ultraviolet-resistant fibers, however.

Woven fabrics

Now that the differences in fibers are a bit clearer, let's take a look at the fabric varieties into which they are woven.

Body cloth

Body cloth is a trade term referring primarily to woven fabrics for seat covering. If side panels are cloth upholstered, they are probably body cloth, too, or a similar cloth of lighter weight. Since side panel covering doesn't receive the wear and stress the seat covers do, you can get by with a lighter material. With most materials, the price difference is small, but if what you've chosen for seats is quite expensive, such as wool, check into a lighter, less costly material for the side panels to harmonize with, if not exactly match, the seats. You might save quite a few dollars.

Body cloth appears in a broad spectrum of colors, patterns and finishes. The main difference in finish is between the napped fabric group, the "fuzzy" ones, and the flat woven fabrics. Each may be known by other specific terms, including a manufacturer's style name, so don't count on any two trimmers being in total agreement on fabric terminology.

Velvet and velour

By definition, *velour* is a French name for velvet. The two are essentially the same fabric, so take your choice of which term to use.

Velvet is a thick, short, warp pile fabric, which means the pile is woven in the lengthwise direction of the fabric, or along the warp threads, as opposed to the woof, or filler, threads which run across. When a piece of velvet is held at the top, the pile will lie down, which is the direction it must be installed.

Crushed velvet is a variation of velvet which has a random, mottled pattern. While material is still hot from the manufacturing process, it is wadded up and put into a large container, where it is compressed, literally crushed. Wrinkles are permanently set into the surface, and the distinctive finish is the result.

Mohair

From the 1920s through the 1940s, when synthetics began to take over, mohair was the most common seat upholstery material in lower- and medium-priced cars. Originally mohair referred to the hair of the Angora goat, pile woven with a medium-length nap. Eventually the term was applied to any wool cloth with a similar weave.

Mohair is still obtainable, but there is so little demand for it that it's quite expensive. Color selection is also narrow, restricted to beige, gray and taupe from some sources. The principal application of mohair is in authentic restoration work. Synthetic material, at about one-third the cost, provides nearly the same feel and appearance, except for the characteristic synthetic sheen.

Bedford cord

This term may crop up among some old-timers. It is a variety of broadcloth named for the town in which it was first woven, New Bedford, Massachusetts. It has ribs, or cords, running in one direction with a nap like velvet. It is smooth, soft and comfortable.

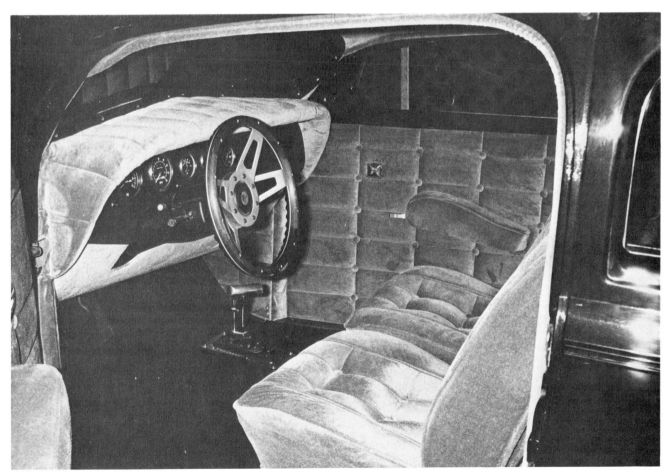

Synthetics now closely simulate mohair at considerably less cost. The nap is slightly longer than that of velour and velvet.

Fabric woven into a ribbed surface is known as corduroy.

While it is possible to get authentic Bedford cord from sources supplying the restoration trade, it is very expensive, like other wool fabrics. Acceptable, even preferable, alternatives are synthetics with a corduroy weave in a range of cord widths. Velvets are also woven in alternating colors or shades to create cord-like designs.

Brocade

Brocade is a flat-woven material with a design in the weave, often slightly raised. The design may also be in a different color or thread to heighten the two-

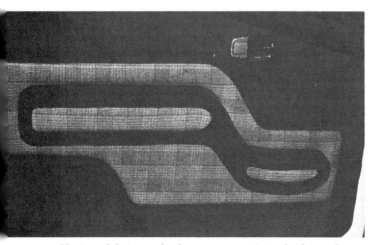

Various fabrics and colors are woven into plaids, as shown, and other patterns. The plaid pattern insert of this street rod door panel offers a contrasting highlight to the plain, dark velour on the rest of the panel.

tone appearance. Chevrolet Impalas and Caprices have often been trimmed with brocade materials.

Tweed

A coarse-woven material, true tweed was originally wool, but now tweed-type fabric is made of synthetic materials, too. It is characterized by a mottled design of different colors and shades. The coarseness of tweed thread makes it prone to snagging, on seats in particular.

Headliner

Fabric suppliers usually single out headliner material, although it may be very similar to body cloth. Not being subjected to stress or wear, headliner material is lighter in weight and in many new cars is not intended to match the rest of the interior, but simply coordinate with it. Many "stock" patterns and materials are available, along with replacement material for most recent-model cars.

Nylon is the most common fiber in cloth headliners, either flat woven or napped. A lot of headlining material is vinyl, which is often perforated or patterned for special effect. You don't have to buy headliner material for the headliner; the material for seats and side panels is acceptable. The considerations are weight and relative cost. Is the material unnecessarily heavy and hard to work with, and would a less expensive fabric serve as well? You'll probably consume four yards of it for a sedan headliner without any fancy work.

There are other specific types of weaves and finishes that appear in auto upholstery. Other identifying terminology describes the patterns, such as plaids, checks, stripes, herringbone and hound's-tooth. Any of these may be offered in either napped or flat woven fabric and in one, two or several colors.

The best way to choose is to keep in mind the kind of fiber you prefer, then spend some time looking at an upholsterer's sample book, being sure to stick with materials suited for automotive applications.

Vinyl

During the synthetic revolution of the 1950s, custom car owners boasted of having a fully rolled and pleated interior of Naugahyde, and manufacturers touted interior materials with exotic names. All were simply different types of vinyl.

Vinyl is the name applied to a group of chemical compounds derived from ethylene to form plastics and resins. The rigid plastics used in dashboards and trim are one form of vinyl; the soft, leatherlike materials used for seat coverings are another.

Although we talk about upholstery material being vinyl, the actual vinyl is the flexible plastic layer on top of a cloth backing. The first product of this type had a coating of a nitrocellulose compound on a coarse, woven cotton backing. Developed as a substitute for leather, it was known as "leather-cloth" or "leather-ette."

Leatherette was subject to cracking and didn't stretch, so its applications were limited. It was replaced by vinyl, which first appeared in cars in 1947 as a flexible plastic coating on a cloth backing. In the early 1950s, U.S. Rubber Co. (now UniRoyal) introduced its trade-named Naugahyde, which had the vinyl coating applied to a stretchable knit backing for greater flexibility and broader application. The name, which came from Naugatuck, Connecticut, the location of UniRoyal's plant, has become so common that it is seldom capitalized anymore and applies to any knit-backed vinyl material.

The industry has continued to develop better varieties of vinyls, and so those available now are far superior to the original materials of the 1950s. The main criticism of vinyl seat covers has always been that they are uncomfortable to sit on; they don't absorb moisture, so riders become sweaty in hot weather. But now there are breathable vinyls with thousands of invisible pores which let air pass through and help keep passengers cool. Other vinyl coverings have larger holes in them as part of the design, which also improves airflow and comfort.

Vinyl has remained a favorite material both for manufacturers and for custom upholsterers for more

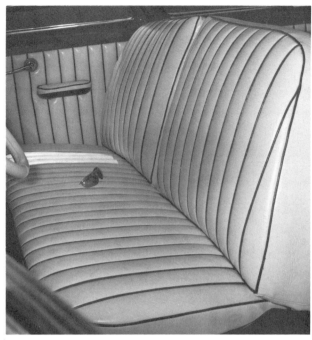

Good wear plus a variety of colors and grain patterns keep vinyl popular.

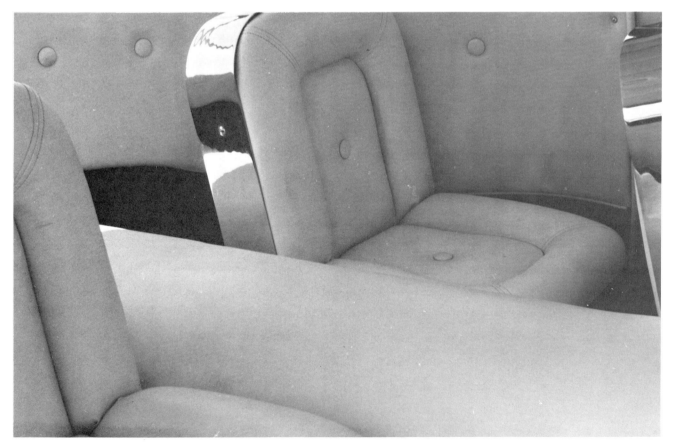

Vinyl consists of a flexible plastic surface over a woven cloth backing.

than thirty years, because it is relatively inexpensive, fairly strong and flexible and can be offered in an infinite variety of colors and grain patterns. Since the vinyl coating, and usually the fabric backing, too, are synthetic, it is immune to rotting and decay. The newest products retain their color well and resist cracking and peeling.

The main drawbacks to vinyl continue to be its lack of absorbency and the fact that it can become very hot in the summer and cold in the winter, and is therefore uncomfortable to sit on.

Vinyl has a place in all phases of custom auto upholstery—seat coverings, door and side panels and headliners. Its serviceability and ease of working and sewing make it ideal for all the little extra spots like the kick panels below the dash, sun visors, rear package shelf and trunk compartment panels. On custom show cars it's also been found dressing up the underhood area, wheelwells and undercarriage.

The strength and wear resistance of vinyl also make it useful as trim. Leather or cloth seats will of-ten have vinyl sidewalls and beading. Door and side panels may be all or part vinyl in either cloth or leather interiors.

Leather

Leather is the one upholstery material that has always been around and probably always will be. Carriage and buggy seats were upholstered in leather long before cars were invented. Its popularity may rise and wane, but except for improvements in processing and finishing, the quality of leather remains constant.

The finest cars have always had leather upholstery. It has superior strength and the look and feel of luxury—and the extra cost can be justified in a luxury car. In the classic era, some top-of-the-line car interiors had leather everywhere, even underneath the cowl and as binding on the carpet. Now its most common application is on the wear surfaces of the seats.

Just as in the interiors of luxury production automobiles, many of the finer custom interiors have re-

Leather is still the choice for the highest-quality upholstery jobs but is recommended only for the experienced trimmer. Larry McDaniel finished John Tober's 1934 Ford phaeton with a combination of plain and perforated leather in an oxblood color.

lied upon leather; it is often specified by the discriminating. Good leather is fairly easy to work with and can be sewn into any style and pattern the owner desires.

But good leather does not come cheaply. That's the reason it is found only in the more expensive custom and production cars. Leather is not in short supply; as a by-product of the meat industry, plenty of the raw product is available. But the process of turning it into a usable upholstery material is long and involved.

Practically all the leather for automotive upholstery is cowhide, although the hides of pigs, goats, horses, deer and other animals are also tanned and made into leather for other applications. The series of operations begins with washing the hide, removing the flesh and hair, and then scrubbing in chemicals that remove any remaining animal protein and agents used in the hair removal process. Finally the hide is "pickled," or washed in a weak acid solution in preparation for tanning.

The tanning process converts the hide into a stable, durable material that will have a long service life. The modern process resulting in a uniform, durable product involves chrome sulfate as the tanning agent in a two-stage procedure.

After tanning, the hide proceeds through the currying process of soaking, splitting, dressing and coloring. The splitting procedure is literally a slicing of the hide by a special machine to yield a material of uniform thickness, usually 1.3 mm for automotive upholstery, while the rougher inside layer that was next to the flesh goes on to become suede for clothing and other products. Thus "top-grain" leather or cowhide refers to the top layer of the hide, not necessarily to quality.

The next step, retanning, is done with an oak extract called tannic acid or tannin, which gives the process its name. Fatliquoring is a chemical process that applies a degree of softness to the leather according to its intended use. The hide is then dried and mechanically softened through controlled flexing and stretching. If the surface needs to be smoothed, it is sanded or buffed. The highest-quality leather requires no buffing and is called "full top grain."

The best coloring method is vat dying, in which the entire hide is soaked in a colored dye; but this is

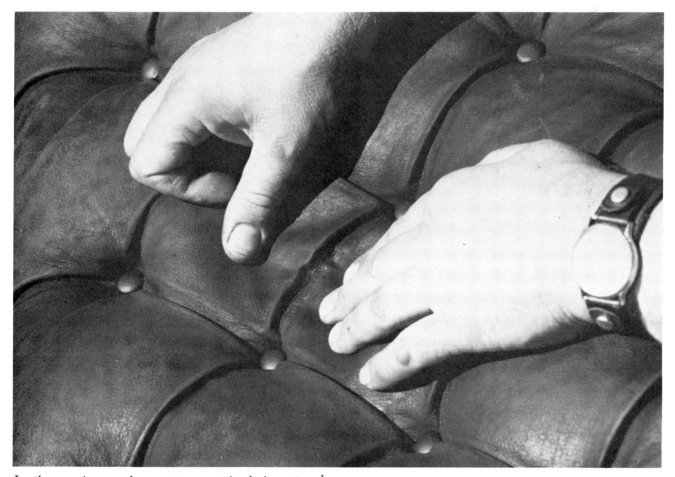

Leather requires regular care to prevent its drying out and splitting.

also very expensive and is seldom done for automotive leather. A hide that is the same color on both sides has been vat dyed, whereas one that is colored on the outside and natural (tan) on the inside has had the color sprayed on. Vat dying produces a uniform tone and, since the color goes all the way through, it tends to hide minor cracks and abrasions. Sprayed-on finishes have been greatly improved in recent years, however.

Surface coloring follows the final buffing step. Often a grain pattern is embossed into the surface at this time, too. Both vat-dyed and spray-finished leathers have a protective top finish coat applied over the color to prevent the color from rubbing off on clothes, and to resist staining and cracking.

Occasionally a car owner or manufacturer boasts of his or her Connolly leather upholstery, and with justification. Connolly Brothers of London is not only the world's largest supplier of upholstery leather, they are also one of the oldest, having been in business for well over 100 years. Connolly has a reputation for producing high-quality hides with uniform color, finish and texture. Prices for Connolly leather depend upon exchange rates, but because of its volume, the company is often competitive with U.S. suppliers.

If you're shopping for leather, look for the company's brand name stamped on the back side of the hide. Reputable suppliers from every country maintain a certain standard of quality and are proud to identify their products. Stay away from unbranded hides. Some cut-rate suppliers shortcut the tanning processes to market a product inferior in flexibility and uniformity, resistance to staining and cracking, and from which the color dye may rub off onto your clothes.

Unlike materials that are manufactured or woven in uniform widths, rolled and sold by the yard, leather is sold by the hide or half hide and priced by the square foot. Hides are just as they came from the cow, which means irregular in shape and variable in size. An average-size full hide will be around forty-five square feet. The range is from thirty-two to fifty-five square feet.

For the sake of estimation, one or two hides will probably cover the seating surfaces of a pair of low-back bucket seats, and two or three should do the seats and cockpit of a street roadster. To cover the front and rear seats of a full-size street rod or custom will require four to seven full hides, more if you're going to have lots of pleats or tufts.

If you have the opportunity to choose your own leather, inspect it carefully for small holes, which may have been caused by flies when the animal was alive and scratches from the barbs of wire fences out on the range. Near the edge, these imperfections won't bother much, but if they're in the middle and you have to make your cuts around them, you can wind up wasting too much material.

Finally, before tackling a leather interior job, be sure you have plenty of practice on vinyl or some scrap material of similar texture. Leather is simply too expensive to experiment on, and every stitch hole in the material is there for good. There's no going back to repair a cobbled job.

Chapter Three

Supplies and tools

Choosing the covering material for your custom interior job is an important decision. You'll be riding on it, looking at it, cleaning it and caring for it for the next several years.

But there are many other important materials, too. The padding on the seats will affect how comfortable and long-lasting they are. The durability and appearance of door and side panels will be affected by the panel material to which the upholstery is attached and the fasteners or adhesives used to attach it.

Upholstery supply firms are found mostly in larger cities. A smaller number of them specialize in automotive upholstery than in furniture upholstery, although many of the supplies and even some of the fabrics apply to both. The problem is that these large wholesalers deal only with established trim shops, not with individuals.

Some mail-order firms serving the hobbyist are listed in the Appendix. Otherwise, contact a local trimmer to purchase the following specialized supplies you need.

At one time, the popular roll-and-pleat design was made by sewing each pleat to a backing material, leaving the roll loose. Each roll was then individually stuffed with cotton batting or wads of horsehair, pushed through with a yardstick or similar device. When all the rolls were filled uniformly, the ends were sewn up and finished off.

While that method can still be followed, chemistry has made it a whole lot easier to do the job with better materials. Whereas cotton batting once was layered to provide the proper padding atop seat

New cotton batting can be stuffed into holes in the coarse material covering seat springs. Batting is intended to be torn to shape and size, not cut.

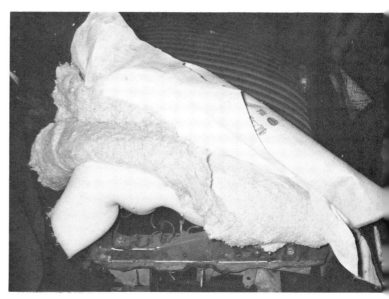

Seat padding consists of a layer of foam rubber covered with cotton batting. The cover material is attached to a thin foam backing.

springs, and more was stuffed in wad by wad to fill out the tufts of seat covering, foam rubber has taken over most of that role. But cotton is still in the picture, along with Dacron, another of its substitutes.

Sprung seats should have three layers of padding. The first, an inexpensive cotton batting, serves as a cushion over the springs and a foundation for the springier padding to come. Placed over the burlap that covers the springs, it evens out any high or low spots.

The second tier provides most of the support and the resilience. Made of foam, it may be shaped and built up as necessary. Finally, there is a relatively thin top layer of soft foam or Dacron batting to provide a smooth surface for the finish covering.

Cotton

Cotton batting comes in sheets usually an inch thick, twenty-seven inches wide and rolled into a bundle. It is easily torn to the size and shape to fit the seat cushion or back. (Other upholstered pieces have simpler construction and low stress, making cotton padding unnecessary.) Cotton mats down to about one-fourth its original thickness within a few months, continuing to function as a foundation, but not contributing to fullness.

Dacron polyester

This synthetic material has replaced some of the cotton (and formerly, wool) batting in upholstery, and it is an acceptable substitute if you don't want to buy both for your project. Dacron's most popular size is one inch thick and twenty-seven inches wide with thirty-nine to forty-five yards of material in a roll, but you can buy smaller amounts from an upholstery shop. It is very soft and compressible, retaining more springiness than cotton, but eventually matting down in the same way. It is a fine final-surface padding, providing a desired resilience as long as it is not compressed by having the cover pulled too tightly. Wads of Dacron are also valuable to fill out spots where the cover may be too loose.

While both are made of Dacron fiber, the Dacron batting or wrap is a totally different product from Dacron woven into a soft, smooth-finish cover fabric.

Foam

The foams found in the upholstery industry, although often referred to as foam rubber, are actually plastics by virtue of the process of their manufacture. I will refer to them simply as foam in this discussion.

You will need to be concerned with two properties of foam: density and firmness. Density, measured in pounds per cubic foot (PCF), indicates the thickness of the cell walls which contain the air pockets that give foam its springiness. A higher PCF number means thicker cell walls and longer life. The seating foam you'll be concerned with will be in the range of 1.4 to 2.0 PCF.

Foam with a density rating of under 1.20 PCF will have a relatively short life, 1.40 to 1.60 PCF mod-

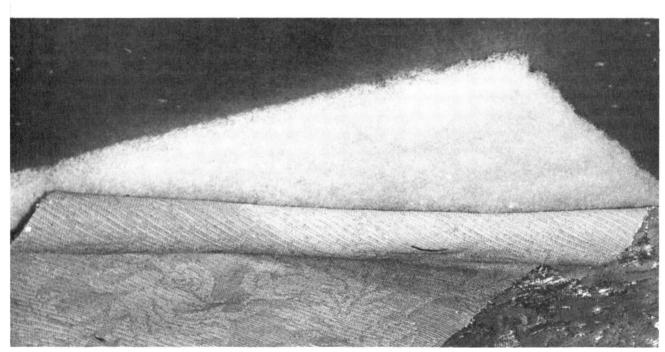

Dacron or polyester filling sometimes replaces cotton batting for padding and filler. Besides being applied in sheets *like this, it can be torn into pieces and stuffed in as needed for fill.*

erate longevity, and 1.80 to 2.0-plus the greatest longevity.

The measure of firmness, or load-bearing capacity, is known as indentation load deflection (ILD) and gauges how much the foam compresses under a given weight. The higher the ILD rating, the firmer the foam, but interpretation varies with the use of the foam.

For seatbacks, an ILD rating of 12 to 14 is considered soft, 16 to 18 medium, 20 to 24 firm and 26 and above extra firm. On the seat cushion, 20 to 24 is soft, 26 to 30 medium, 32 to 36 firm, 38 to 45 extra firm and 46 and above super firm.

Firmness and density should be carefully considered when constructing or repadding seats. For most of your work, two different grades, one of medium to hard firmness for supportive padding and buildup and a softer one for finish padding, should be sufficient. Those with a higher density rating are preferable for seating, but not as necessary for padding door and side panels.

Foam rubber comes in various thicknesses and densities, and is easily cut with a hacksaw blade. Greater thicknesses are created by gluing two or more sheets together.

Late model seats have one-piece foam cushions molded to the shape of the seat frame. This front bucket seat is from an Olds Cutlass.

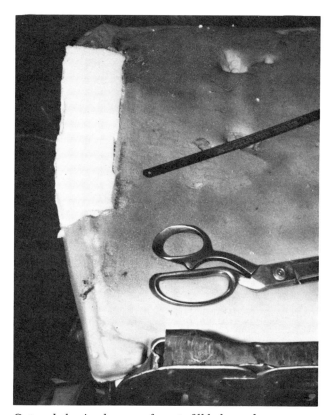

Cut and glue in place new foam to fill holes and worn areas. Trim the edges of the hole so they're nearly square, then cut foam to fit, adding layers as necessary to fill the hole. Trimming the foam to the seat's exact contour isn't necessary as the foam will conform to the shape as the cover is attached.

Foam comes in a variety of forms. Thinner sheets up to one inch are rolled, while thicker forms come in blocks two to five (or even more) inches thick. Since foam is manufactured in huge "buns," it can be sliced to any size and thickness. For your work, a supply of soft one-inch foam will be needed for surface padding. Rather than buying several sizes of firmer material, get a sufficient quantity of one-inch or two-inch blocks. They can be layered to create the desired thickness.

To make upholstery jobs even easier, foam padding is provided in a variety of special forms. Some comes premolded in channels of various widths to facilitate laying out and sewing up a roll-and-pleat design.

Foam in 1/4 inch and 1/2 inch thicknesses is available with a light muslin or paper backing attached. A backing is necessary when padding must be sewn to hold the thread, which will pull through plain foam.

Cloth-backed foam can be made at home by gluing a thin sheet of foam to a woven cloth such as muslin, or even to an old bed sheet or window curtain. A

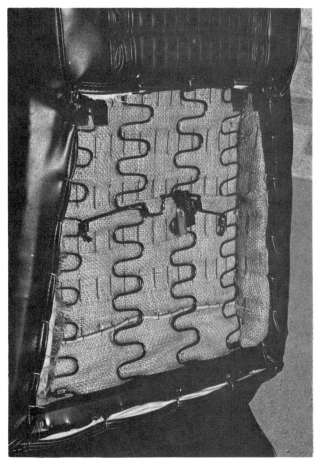

Strong and coarse, burlap keeps springs from damaging padding. Pull it over and attach it to the frame with hog rings to form a base for the padding.

thickness of 1/2 inch next to the outside covering is sufficient for most purposes. It affords enough padding to give definition to a sewn-in design or pattern.

If you're working with seats from a fairly recent-model car, they may have a molded foam padding set into some sort of frame or frame-and-spring combination. Molded foam may be rejuvenated and puffed up to restore its shape and resiliency by applying steam with a steamer, teakettle or steam iron to areas that have stiffened. Be careful not to touch a hot iron or utensil to the foam, as it will melt.

Chunks of the molded cushion may be fragmented or torn out; these often are in high-wear areas like the outside edges of the driver's seat. Cut out such a spot to provide even surfaces on all sides. Then cut a piece of foam of similar density to fit the hole, and glue it into place.

Burlap

The need for a tough, inexpensive material to cover seat springs, preventing their flexing from shifting or damaging the padding, is filled by burlap. This coarse, natural material is sold in rolls; old potato sacks that have been cleaned will also serve the purpose.

Good seats that don't require rebuilding or replacement of springs probably won't need new burlap. If yours do, pay attention to how the old material was fitted and attached, and put on the new in the same way. Usually it is pulled snugly over the springs, wrapped over the outside rim of the seat frame and attached to it with hog rings.

Panel board

For door and side panels, upholstery covering must be attached to a strong, rigid backing. One type of panel board is made especially for this purpose. Waterproof panel board, treated to keep its shape if it becomes wet, is recommended. Some upholsterers prefer 1/8 inch Masonite to panel board. Wood paneling made for finishing walls in a house is another alternative. If you're concerned about the effects of moisture or humidity, seal whatever panel board you choose with two or three coats of a preservative (such as Thompson Water Seal or Weldwood Woodlife).

Provided you've been able to salvage them, the old panels or backing from your car can serve as patterns to shape the new boards. If not, make patterns out of heavy, clear plastic held or taped to the door or panel, drawn with a marker and cut out. Upholstery shears or tin snips will suffice for cutting panel board, but a saber saw or jigsaw will be required for Masonite or wood.

Welting

A welt is a small roll or bead which adds strength to a seam or edge, or decorates or highlights a design in the fabric cover. Welt cord in white plastic, a tissue material or jute is made in sizes from $3/32$ inch to $6/32$ inch. This core is then covered with matching or contrasting cover material. Simpler to install, however, is finished welt cord, which comes in a variety of colors and fabric selections to harmonize with your interior design.

Windlace

Windlace, the roll that forms a seal around door openings, is normally covered with upholstery fabric to match and blend with the sidewalls. Supply houses offer it in rolls covered in many popular fabrics and colors to match the newer model cars, as well as antique taupe and gray. There's a good chance you can find a ready-made windlace to go with your upholstery choice. If not, you'll have to buy windlace rubber core material, which comes in rolls, and cover it with your upholstery material.

Adhesives

For the amount of work you'll be doing, a spray can or two of adhesive should be sufficient. Be sure to get a product made for interior trimming (such as 3M General Trim Adhesive or Camie Spray Adhesive). If you plan to do more trim work, you may want to investigate a hot glue gun or an air compressor–operated glue-spraying system.

Ready-to-install welt cord can be found in a variety of materials and colors. It has a sewing allowance of about $3/8$ inch and cuts about every $1/4$ inch to facilitate forming it around corners.

Panel board can be cut with heavy shears or a utility knife.

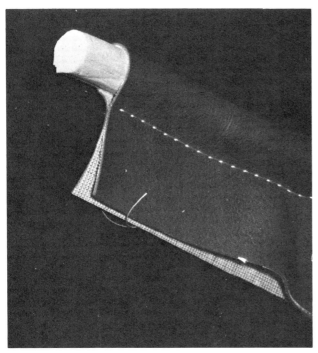

Windlacing is available ready-made or you can make it by gluing and sewing material around a rubber core. A welting foot on the sewing machine is required to place the seam tight against the rubber core.

A pneumatic staple gun like this one is handy, but a manual one will work as well.

Tools

Basic mechanic and household tools you already have, such as pliers, screwdrivers, tack hammer, electric drill and saber saw, will be needed for this job. A good pair of upholstery shears is a necessity for the amount of cutting required; household scissors just aren't adequate.

Although a wooden yardstick will suffice, a steel straightedge up to five feet long will make marking easier; a large square is valuable, too. Chalk shaped into a sharp wedge is fine for marking dark material; a soft lead pencil is useful for lighter shades. Tailor's chalk is also available. Don't use a ballpoint pen on a cover material, as the ink will bleed through.

A razor-blade cutter or hobby knife will be needed to cut foam and for other trimming. An electric carving knife (Don't let your spouse catch you!) works great for cutting and shaping blocks of foam, but a hacksaw blade is also good. Hog-ring pliers are necessary for attaching the rings that hold seat covers on. A $1/4$ inch punch is useful for cutting holes in panel board for trim and hardware. An awl or ice pick is handy to locate holes through fabric and to punch holes for buttons and trim. If you don't have a staple gun, plan to rent one for the side panel work.

Hardware and fasteners

When dismantling your car's interior in preparation for its new trim job, be sure to keep all the clips, trim screws, tacks and other fasteners you remove. Put them in separate containers and identify them. Even if they're not reusable, you will know exactly what to get as replacements. Some common fasteners will be obtainable at a hardware store, while you may need to get some specialized items from an upholstery shop or supplier.

Get a supply of staples for your staple gun to attach covering to panel boards. For strength, use the longest staples you can that don't go entirely through the panel board. Early-style street rod bodies usually have wood reinforcement to which upholstery is stapled or tacked. A supply of $3/4$ inch hog rings will be needed for attaching seat covering. Some long upholsterer's pins are handy for pinning material together before sewing.

Newer seats, except those made with molded foam padding, have zigzag springs, known as sinuous or no-sag, for cushion support. Earlier cars had coil springs joined together into cushion units. Both types are available from upholstery supply houses, if needed, to replace ones that are broken or sagging from years of wear.

For an interior design calling for buttons, you'll want to look into a button-making machine, which starts at under $100, and a supply of button molds. Popular sizes are from $9/16$ inch to one inch in diameter. Some suppliers will make buttons to order at prices from seventy-five cents and up, or you may pay an upholstery shop to make them.

Nylon thread is recommended for your sewing jobs, although Dacron thread is also good. You'll need a spool of hand sewing thread and at least one good curved needle for hand finishing. Thread comes in a variety of colors to blend with your covering material. You may also need nylon tufting twine for tying in buttons.

Sewing machine

This is the item, more than any other, that usually prevents automotive hobbyists from tackling their own upholstery jobs. Upholstery means sewing, something they may know nothing about and have little interest in learning. The image that's conjured up is of a large, expensive commercial sewing machine.

That's not necessarily the case. Many of the popular cloth fabrics are light enough to be sewn on a good-quality home machine adapted for the job with a heavy-duty needle and presser foot. Leather and vinyl will require a stronger machine, however. One of the suppliers listed in the Appendix offers a reasonably priced compact machine that will handle most upholstery tasks.

What you're after, besides the capacity to sew several layers of heavy material or sew through panel board, is a walking foot, which helps pull the material through the machine. A welting foot, which permits stitching right up next to welt cord or windlace core, is a useful option if you'll be making quite a bit of piping. A reverse setting on the machine can also be convenient for intricate stitching, but isn't a necessity.

Much of the upholstery job can be done without sewing. Covering can be glued or stapled onto door and side panels. A headliner need not require sewing. Carpet edging can be done by hand. The only place a sewing machine is a necessity is for seat covers, and even at that, it is possible to make some seat coverings on a plywood base without sewing.

Some sewing machine dealers and equipment-rental firms have commercial machines to rent for the necessary sewing. If you have everything ready ahead of time, the cost will not be prohibitive. The alternative is to lay out your seat covering and take it to a commercial shop to be sewn up.

Whatever the choice, don't let the lack of an industrial sewing machine deter you from doing your own upholstery work.

Work area

A fairly large and clean work area is a must for any upholstery job, so you can lay out large sheets of material for measuring, marking and cutting. Close proximity to the car isn't necessary, but it is helpful when measuring and fitting pieces individually. A 4 × 8 foot panel of 1/2 inch plywood set over a pair of sawhorses in the garage would provide an adequate work area, but be sure to clean or cover the floor to prevent soiling of your material. A board laid over a pool table or Ping-Pong table may also serve as a work site.

Make a checklist of the materials and supplies you'll require and have everything on hand so your job won't be delayed while you wait for a needed component or tool.

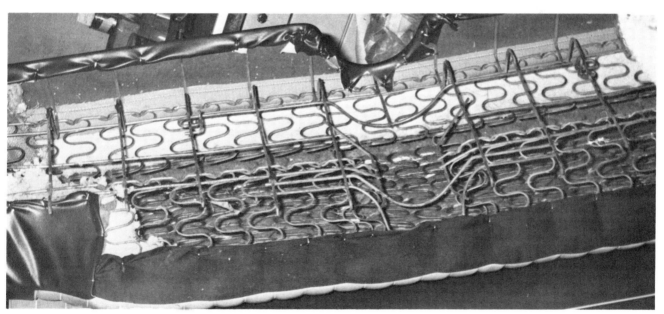

Some new sinuous, zigzag springs may be required to rebuild seats.

Chapter Four

Upholstery techniques

Upholstering, like most crafts, is a matter of learning a few basic procedures, then applying them in various combinations to create a finished product. Once learned, the basic techniques of working with upholstery fabric to create patterns and designs can be applied to making seat covers, sidewall panels, headliners and other decorative components.

With all upholstering tasks, step one is to make a pattern, step two is to prepare the covering, and step three is to fit and attach it to the panel or seat. Since pleating, tufting and other design techniques discussed in this chapter have to do with making the covering, we'll deal only with that here. Except in instances in which the cover is constructed directly on the panel, applying the covering to the various interior components will be taken up in subsequent chapters.

Preparation

If you are contemplating totally refinishing the interior, the place to start is with the removal of all the old upholstery. This step as it applies to specific parts of the interior is discussed in more detail in the chapters covering those areas, so it would be a good idea to look ahead to those sections before tearing into the task. If you're not doing a total job, remove only those parts being refinished plus any that restrict access to them.

The interior work must be done in a logical sequence so you don't find yourself having to tear out something because you forgot to put something else in first. You also need to allow yourself as much working space as possible. In addition, you need to establish exactly what parts are to be finished with what materials, make a pattern for each individual part and, from the patterns collectively, determine how much material the job will require.

Take the seats out first. They don't necessarily have to be dismantled at this point. Remove trim and garnish moldings to expose the attachment of the headliner and side panels. Remove these and the door panels, being careful to note how they are attached, and save all clips and fasteners. Remove the kick panels, package shelf and any other parts, and remove the carpet last, as it provides a soft surface to work on and catches any screws you drop.

When dismantling, keep track of how parts and upholstery attach, such as this headliner glued around the rear windows. Some installations may also have staples or tacks in this area.

Make a pattern

Like a good dressmaker, you should begin your interior layout by making patterns of each part and panel to be upholstered. For a start, separate all the individual pieces at the seams and identify each one with a code, such as FSC for front seat cushion and FSB for front seatback. Number the headliner panels from front to rear. If some pieces are to be finished in

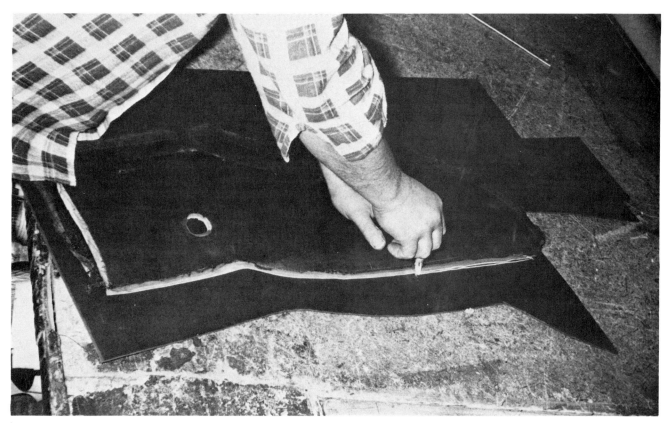

Make a pattern from each old piece that is removed. Use a rigid piece like this side panel board wherever available. Ar- *range the patterns according to the type of covering to be made for them.*

one type of fabric and others in another, separate and stack them accordingly. These pieces may serve as patterns, provided they are in reasonable shape and not shrunken.

The other, possibly preferable, approach to pattern making is to roll out a length of heavy paper and trace the perimeter outline of each piece onto it with an indelible marker. For two kinds or colors of fabric, make the patterns on brown wrapping paper for one and on white butcher paper for the other. Identify each part and, if it's a factor, the direction the cover has to lie. It may be easier to trace around a rigid panel than its cover.

If there is no old piece to serve as a pattern, cover that section with a heavy piece of clear plastic and trace the outline onto it with a marker, including any openings and attachment points. Mark the locations of hardware such as door handles, window cranks and decorative trim on your paper patterns. If placement of a design will be a factor, draw in the side-to-side and top-to-bottom center lines of each panel, too.

Now proceed to sketch your design onto the pattern or onto another sheet of paper. Using a pencil at first allows you to erase and make changes until the layout is satisfactory. Then it can be traced over with the marker.

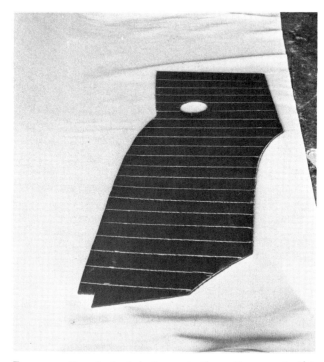

Draw a roll-and-pleat design onto the pattern or, in this case, the panel board to be covered.

61

Popular velour materials need to be installed so the nap lies down. This gives it a uniform appearance and minimizes the tendency for it to catch dirt and dust.

If a design such as rolls and pleats or tufting is involved, it should be drawn onto the pattern first, with careful measurement to make the design come out even and centered. Further discussion of these elements will follow. Determine where sections of different materials or colors will go, and put them onto the pattern with markers of corresponding colors.

When you work out a particular measurement, such as the width of rolls or depth of a certain panel, write it on the pattern for quick reference later. Make notes in the margin to remind you of other points to consider when making up the upholstery cover. Having a pattern for every piece will ensure that nothing is overlooked.

Estimate material requirements

Your patterns will be your best tool for making an accurate determination of the amounts of material (padding as well as cover fabric) your job will take. Place all the pieces to come out of one type of fabric onto another large sheet of paper, and arrange them to make the best use of the material with a minimum of waste. Most fabric comes in fifty-four-inch widths, so make your layout that wide. When all the parts are accounted for on this model, measurement of the length covered gives you the number of yards of fabric required.

Get one or two yards extra to give yourself a margin for error in cutting; allow more, too, for pleats or tufts. For example, a seat cushion fifty-four inches wide may require seventy-two inches of material for deep tufts or pleats. As a rough idea, front and rear seats together require ten to twelve yards of material,

a headliner four or five yards and an entire sedan interior twenty to twenty-five yards.

Something else to bear in mind before cutting or sewing is any "direction" consideration of your fabric. If it has nap, such as velvet, run your hand over it to determine in which direction the nap lies. Stroked one way it is smooth and velvety, the other way coarse and bristly. Stroking a cat has the same effect; the fur lies down smooth when you pet it head to toe, but stroked "backwards," the fur goes in all directions and results in an irritated cat!

For the color and sheen to look correct and uniform, a napped fabric must be applied so that the nap falls down like the flow of a waterfall. It feels smooth when stroked from top to bottom on side panels and seatbacks and from back to front on seat cushions. It stays cleaner, too, because it tends to shed, rather than trap, dust and soil.

Vinyl may have a particular grain pattern that gives it direction, so be sure the pattern is applied in the same direction on all panels. Most vinyl stretches more in one direction than another, so this is a factor in how it's applied. Like vinyl, leather may have an embossed pattern that will determine the direction it should be installed.

Unless you have some experience working with fabrics and performing the procedures that follow, it would be wise to do some practicing with scrap material such as an old sheet before attempting it with upholstery cloth. It is also helpful to make a small paper "model" of the piece to follow—anything to avoid a mistake that could ruin a piece of expensive fabric.

Rolls and pleats

Throughout the years rolls and pleats have been the most popular upholstery design. For a finished custom car in the 1950s, an interior of Naugahyde or leatherette rolls and pleats was a must. Rolls and pleats have a multitude of variations, too.

Tuck-and-roll is another term for this design. So is channeling, although it is applied more in the furniture-trimming trade. A pleat is a fold made when the material is turned back upon itself and secured in that position. On a seat cover or headliner, the pleat in the outside covering is sewn to a flexible backing material. On a door or side panel it may be either sewn or stapled to the panel board.

In earlier times the cover fabric was left loose between pleats, then stuffed with cotton or foam rubber. The modern method is to secure the pleat through a sheet of foam to the backing. The foam provides the "puff" of the roll, or channel. The pleat is "tucked" down between the rolls.

Rolls can be any width, from an inch or less to several inches. The most common are between 1½ inches and three inches. Although ordinarily thought of as even and parallel, they can also be done in irregular straight lines, varying widths or curves. Feel free to express your creativity in the roll and pleat design you devise.

The rolls' fullness varies according to the thickness of padding and how each roll is finished. We'll look at several ways, from simple to complex, of making rolls from thin to fat.

Pressed pleats

As mentioned in Chapter 2, some vinyl and cloth fabrics are available with a pleat pattern heat-pressed in. Lots of production vehicles are finished this way, but the fabric choices in the aftermarket are slim.

Installation of a prepleated fabric is the same as that for a flat fabric. Measure the material, being sure the pleat pattern is properly centered, and cut to size with enough of a border to attach to the panel or surrounding material.

Topstitching

While topstitching is quite simple and is practiced widely in the new car industry, it has durability limitations. For one thing, puncturing the cover material by sewing weakens it along the stitch line, and flexing over a period of time may cause it to split. Also, the stitches are holding only one layer, and the thread is exposed to wear.

Topstitching and pressed pleats don't make a true roll-and-pleat job because no pleats are actually folded into the material. However, they do provide the same effect.

Prechanneled foam is the easiest to work with if you can get it in the channel width you want. Then it's simply a matter of marking the face of the cover material with stitch lines to match the channels in the foam, and sewing along them.

If you're starting from scratch, draw the tuck-and-roll design from your paper pattern onto the backing material, a piece of 1/4 inch or 1/2 inch foam and the front, or face, of the cover material. Backing material can be any tightly woven fabric that will hold the stitches. Additional backing is not necessary if you use cloth-backed foam.

Many late-model cars with vinyl upholstery have pressed-in pleats. These Plymouth buckets also have a tooled design along the borders of the pleated panels.

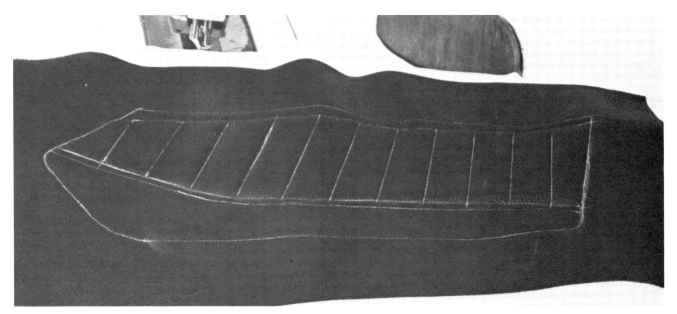

Draw the pattern to be stitched onto the top side of the cover material. For marking, use chalk on dark materials, soft pencil on lighter ones.

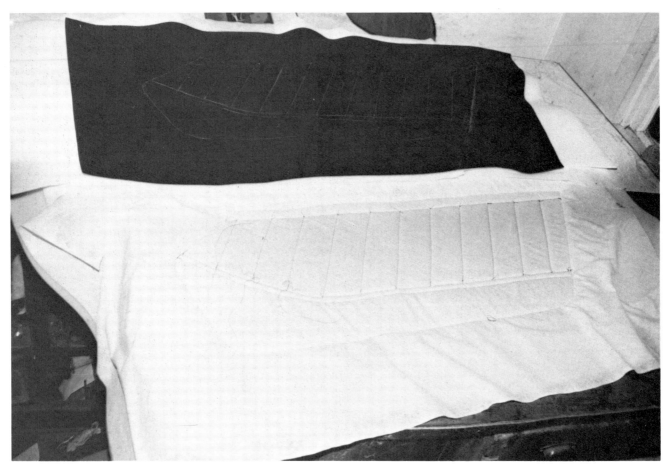

Foam and backing cloth have been sewn together in the same pattern as the cover. The backing here is a paper cloth often used by upholsterers, but muslin or an old bed sheet will also work to hold the stitches.

Draw the stitch lines all the way to the edge of the piece. Beginning in the middle, line up the corresponding lines on the cover, foam and backing and sew along it. Move to the next line and so on to one edge, then return to the center and work out to the other edge. Finally, sew around the outer perimeter of the rolled panel. When it is ready to be joined to another panel, you can trim the edge as necessary to make it easier to work with.

Somewhat sharper definition for the topstitched tuck-and-roll job is possible if the foam is slit with a razor half or three-fourths of the way through (don't cut all the way) and the cover material pressed into the crack before sewing. Hold the slit open with your fingers as you direct the material through the machine, being careful to follow the stitch line marked on the cover.

Some upholsterers topstitch deeper tucks and fuller rolls with foam padding one or two inches thick, following the above approach and slitting the foam to about 1/2 inch from the backing. Starting in the middle, the cover is folded along the marked stitch line and the fold inserted into the slit, tucked down as far as it will go and held with two or three upholsterer's pins. When all tucks are done the same way, they are topstitched by spreading the slit open enough for the material to go through the machine. If your machine will handle it, this is a good method, because the foam closes over the seam, both hiding it and protecting it from wear.

Layout and measurement

The above method and those to follow will require some different measuring, so we'll cover that here before going on to sewn and stapled pleats.

If the foam padding is to be more than 1/2 inch thick, you need to make an allowance for the fullness of the rolls. Cut a strip of the foam the width you want the roll, say 1 1/2 inches, or mark two lines that distance apart on a block of foam. Lay the cover material over it, and have a helper pull the material down tight into the foam exactly on the two marks or around the strip of foam, simulating the arc of the finished roll. Follow the arc with a piece of paper, marking it at the bottom of each depression. Measuring the distance between the marks will tell you how much material to allow for the fullness of each roll.

When pleats are to be sewn or stapled, allow an additional 1/2 inch, the amount needed to fold over and form each pleat. The roll width, 1 1/2 inches, plus 1/2 inch for the pleat, and, say, another 1/2 inch for fullness makes 2 1/2 inches of material required for each roll.

To follow this example through, let's say the panel to be covered is thirty-two inches wide. Thirty-two divided by 1 1/2 inches, the width of each roll, equals twenty-one, the number of rolls to cover the panel (plus a fraction left over at each end). Transfer these measurements to the foam padding. Mark the outside lines thirty-two inches apart (leaving some extra on each end) and the center line, which will be sixteen inches from each end.

If there were to be an even number of rolls in the panel, there would be an equal number on either side of the line. Taking the example of twenty-one rolls, an odd number, the center line falls in the middle of the center roll. The roll, 1 1/2 inches wide, divided by two equals 3/4 inch, the distance on either side of the center line where the first pleats must go. Measure and draw these lines onto the foam. Then measure out in 1 1/2 inch increments in each direction, drawing a parallel line at each point, the location of the pleats.

The same thing must be done with the cover material, but on it the pleats must be 2 1/2 inches apart,

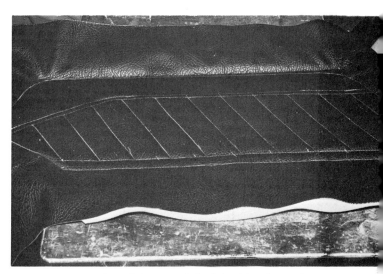

A cover sewn to 1/2 inch foam and cloth backing has only a slight raised-roll effect. This, along with topstitching, gives sufficient definition to panel designs.

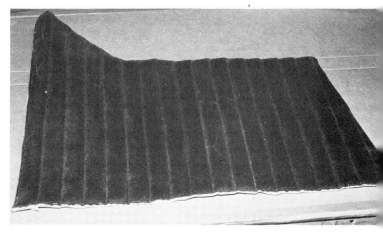

Velour topstitched in narrower channels has a puffier look than the vinyl.

On the back of the cover, mark lines where pleats are to be sewn or stapled. Allow an extra 1/2 inch in addition to the width of the roll for the width of the sewn or stapled pleat.

Cut out cover material. Be sure the top and bottom lines make a one- to two-inch allowance top and bottom, and the width of an extra roll or two on each end and for attachment to the panel.

Draw lines where pleats are to be. The material will be folded on these lines to form the pleats.

Mark pleat lines on the foam backing. These will be the exact width of the desired pleats.

taking into account the allowances for fullness and pleating. Mark the center line of the piece of fabric, then measure out 1¼ inches on either side for the first pleats and in 2½ inch increments in both directions for the remaining pleats. Also draw in the top and bottom line of the pleated panel on both fabric and foam, allowing two inches of border on each side.

Sewn pleats

For sewn pleats, the pleat lines are marked onto the back side of the fabric. Lay the cover material face down on a clean worktable. With a soft lead pencil for light material or chalk for dark, draw lines to indicate the top and bottom edges of the roll-and-pleat panel, then additional lines two inches outside the first to indicate the sewing or attachment allowance. Determine the exact center, side to side, of the piece of material, and draw a line from top to bottom. Measure and draw out your pleat pattern from the center reference point.

Fold the material over on the first pleat line and sew along ⅛ inch from the fold. Continue across the piece, sewing each pleat in the same manner. Then lay the cover over the foam back and line up the sewn pleats with the pleat lines marked on the foam. Working from one end to the other, sew each pleat to the backing. Place the seam no more than ⅛ inch in from the first stitch line. Finally, sew across the top and bottom lines, and the roll-and-pleat panel is ready to attach.

When padding with foam thicker than ½ inch, cut the foam into strips for the individual rolls and follow the procedure outlined in the next section on stapling pleats.

Stapled pleats

Rolls and pleats can be done on side panels by stapling directly to the panel board instead of sewing. Sheet, cloth-backed or prechanneled foam work equally well for padding. Lines designating the pleat locations must be drawn onto the panel board as well as the foam. Follow the procedure outlined above for sewing pleats, but instead of sewing, staple through the cover and foam onto the panel board.

Fold the cover along the pleat line, align the fold with the line on the foam backing and sew ¼ inch from the fold. Begin at the end of the panel that will be most visible, and work across to the other end.

Draw the pleat pattern with 1/2 inch allowance for each pleat onto the back of the cover material, the same as for sewing pleats.

To help maintain a straight line and provide something besides cover for the staples to grip, cut strips of light cardboard the length of the pleats and 1/4 inch wide. Place a strip along each fold and staple down the middle of it at about 1/2 inch intervals when attaching the cover to the panel board.

Beginning at the end of the panel that will be most visible, fold the first pleat and line up the fold with the first pleat line on the panel. Place a 1/4 inch wide strip of light cardboard along the fold to form a straight, even line and provide an additional surface for the staples to grip. Staple down the middle of the strip at 1/2 inch intervals.

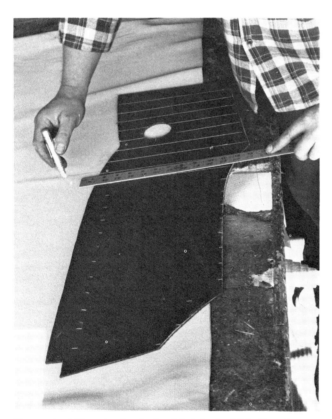

Draw pleat lines in the desired finished width directly onto the panel board. Cut the board to the exact size and shape.

Cut foam into strips the width of the pleats and spray with upholstery adhesive. Also apply adhesive to the panel board. Adhesive works best when allowed to set up until it is tacky on both surfaces.

Another method that's especially useful when padding with thicker or firmer foam is to cut the foam into strips the right width of each roll and slightly longer. Fold the cover material to form the first pleat at the end of the panel that will be most visible. Line up the fold with the corresponding line drawn on the panel board. Place a cardboard strip along the fold and staple down the middle of it.

Apply trim adhesive to one of the foam strips and to the panel board where the first roll goes. Glue the foam strip into place with one edge just covering the stapled cardboard strip and the other lined up with the next mark on the panel board. "Roll" the material over the foam, form the next fold along the next mark in line with the mark on the panel board, and staple down in the same manner as the first. Continue gluing a strip of foam and attaching a pleat at each line across the board.

Finish each end by gluing a strip of foam onto the last section, then pulling the covering snugly over it and around the edge of the panel board. Staple the cover on the back about 1/4 inch from the edge of the board. Pull the cover over the top and bottom edges, making sure any wrinkles are pulled out of the rolls, and staple in the same way. When finished, trim the excess material 1/2 inch from the staple line.

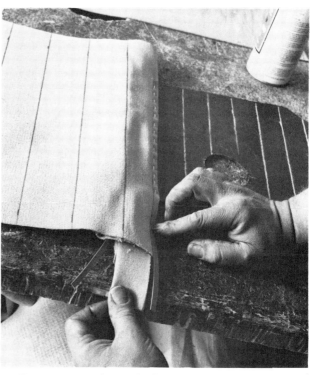

Pull cover material over the foam, make the next pleat and staple to the board with a cardboard strip as before. Foam strips may be left longer than necessary and trimmed later.

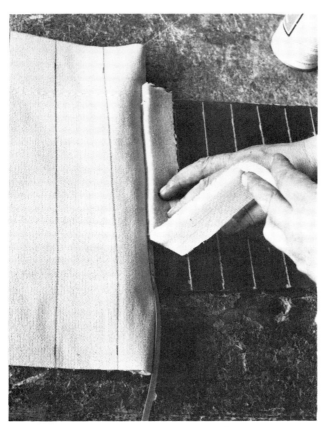

Glue down a strip of foam just covering the previously stapled pleat.

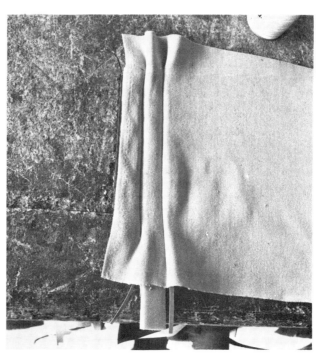

Stapled pleats will look as good as sewn ones when finished. To finish the end, this panel needed a vinyl "tail" added to attach to a tack strip. Otherwise a strip of foam could be glued next to the end and the cover stretched over the edge and stapled on back.

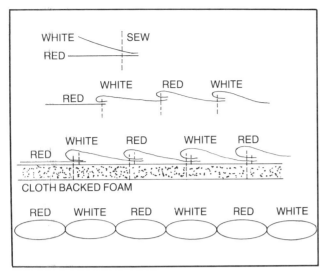

For candy-stripe or alternating color rolls, cut individual strips of material and sew them together. They are then attached to the backing.

Roll-and-pleat variations

"Candy stripe" is a special roll-and-pleat design that was popular for custom cars in the 1950s. You may wish to duplicate the style. It consists of alternating rolls of material in two contrasting colors, such as black, red or blue with white, or light and dark shades of the same color. One very attractive treatment I noticed recently had stripes of dark red, tending toward maroon, alternating with bright red, the dominant interior color.

Another variation on the candy-stripe theme uses thin piping or welting in a contrasting color between rolls. Two-inch rolls in off-white vinyl, for example,

are highlighted by 1/4 inch welts in a darker color to complement the exterior finish of the car.

Both variations are constructed similarly, so I'll cover them together here. To make rolls of alternating colors, cut strips of cover material a few inches longer than needed to cover the panel and the width of each roll plus one inch for attachment. It is helpful to make a paper model to be certain everything fits together as planned.

Place one strip of cover material face up and a strip of the alternate color face to face with it, lining up the two edges. Sew the two strips together. Pull the second strip across, and attach another strip of the first color in the same manner. Continue across the panel.

When the entire panel is finished in alternating stripes, sew it to cloth-backed foam as described for sewn pleats. When working on a side panel, glue strips of foam into place and staple the two cover strips to the board as outlined above.

To add piping to the roll-and-pleat job, cut piping strips slightly longer than the pleats (see instructions for making piping later in this chapter). Follow instructions outlined earlier for sewing pleats, but insert a strip of piping into each pleat. Then sew or staple as close as possible to the welt cord.

Of course, the width and shape of rolls can be varied, too. What it takes is careful measuring and drawing the same pattern on both cover and backing materials. The safest way to make a curved pattern or rolls

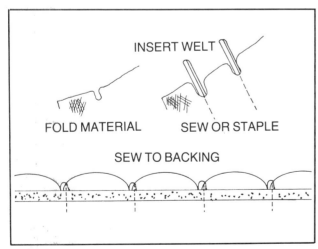

A candy-stripe alternative adds a welt strip in the fold of each pleat. Sew the welt in first, then sew each pleat to backing.

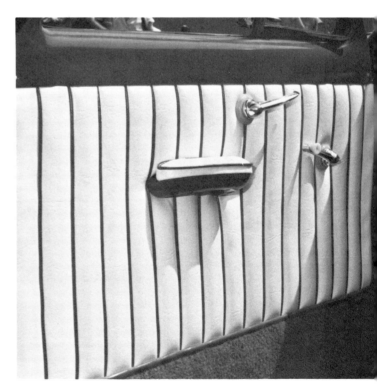

Here, the welt is of a contrasting color to the rolls and pleats.

70

that are wider at one end than the other is to cut them out individually and sew together in the chosen pattern. This way you can control the direction of the nap or fabric pattern if necessary.

Tufting

Tufting has been nearly as popular and versatile as rolls and pleats in custom interior design. Its popularity has risen and waned but has never disappeared completely. Tufting can stand alone as a design or be combined with rolls and pleats and other designs.

Tufting may be done in diamond, half diamond, square or rectangular patterns or variations of them. The points where the lines of the pattern intersect are usually adorned with buttons, which pull the cover material down into the padded backing and give the tuft its fullness. Tufting, or quilting, can also be done without buttons, and conversely, decorative buttons can be added to flat panels or pleats without being part of a tufted design.

Layout and measurement

Designing and laying out the pattern on paper first is particularly critical in making a button-tufting job turn out well. Assuming both seats and side panels will have the same design, the size and shape of tufts must work well for both. You may wish to put the tuft pattern only in inserts surrounded by a roll.

Assemble the measurements of all the surfaces to be covered by tufts. Adopt a scale, such as one inch to one foot, and sketch each surface on a piece of paper. Try drawing an arrangement to see how it looks—for example, three equal-size diamonds across a bucket seat. Experiment with different sizes and arrangements until you're satisfied with one for the seat. Then see how it will work in the same scale on the door and side panels. The design doesn't have to extend all the way to the edge.

Diamond tufts look best when the diamonds are longer than they are wide. A rule of thumb is to make the horizontal dimension between one-half and two-thirds the vertical dimension. For a rectangular pattern, make the rectangles wider than they are high for the most pleasing appearance. Remember that button tufting is time consuming and also takes more material, so don't make your job too taxing or expensive by designing too complex a tuft pattern.

When you're satisfied with the design on paper, transfer the measurements in full scale either to a large paper pattern or directly to a backing material. As with rolls and pleats, locate the center, up and down as well as side to side, and draw these lines across the backing in pencil or chalk for reference.

Lay out the pattern, drawing in the locations of all the buttons and the lines between. Where the design will go and how heavy the padding is will determine how the tufting is accomplished and how much definition the tufts will have.

Creating this fan-shaped pattern in Ed Guffey's 1950 Ford required careful planning and measurement. The design was drawn onto the vinyl cover material, then topstitched through a foam backing to give the rolls depth.

A diamond-tufting pattern adorned with contrasting buttons makes a striking interior scheme in Jerry Johnson's 1954 Olds. Diamonds were topstitched in white vinyl, and green velvet buttons were inserted at the intersections.

Surface design

A button placed at each intersecting point of the pattern may be pulled down to depress the cover into a padded backing. If the backing is 1/4 inch or 1/2 inch cloth-backed foam, the fullness and definition will be slight to moderate. A surface design is sufficient for side panels, full seat covers or seat inserts.

Lay the cover material face up over a piece of foam, and draw your design onto it from your pattern. Allow several inches extra on all sides, and draw center reference lines onto the cover.

For door and side panels, lay out the design on the panel board and drill a 1/4 inch hole at each button location. Lay the cover and foam over the board, line up the design, and punch a hole with an awl through the cover and backing at each button point. Insert buttons with prongs into the holes and bend the prongs over on the back. The edges of the cover may then be pulled over the edges of the panel and stapled.

If a surface design of button tufts is to be a seat cover, the buttons may tie through a thicker layer of padding or through all the seat padding. One method is to cut a piece of foam of the chosen thickness to the shape of the seat surface and glue it to a piece of heavy material like canvas or denim. Position the cover on the foam and secure it with upholsterer's pins. Pierce the cover, foam and backing at each button point with an awl, then, with a needle to pull the attached twine through, insert an eyelet button into each hole. Tie the twine through a shirt button or with a wad of cotton to prevent it from pulling through the canvas backing. When all buttons are in place, tighten them to a uniform height.

If tying buttons through all layers of a seat cushion, follow the same procedure, but tie the button twine to the seat springs or frame.

Pretufted cover

It's worth mentioning here that some cover material is available from fabric suppliers with a diamond, square or rectangular pattern stitched or heat-pressed into it. Some vinyls even have the outlines of buttons pressed in. If the color, type of material, finish and design are in keeping with your interior plan, a prequilted material is worth considering. You can still add decorative buttons in a matching or contrasting color when you install it.

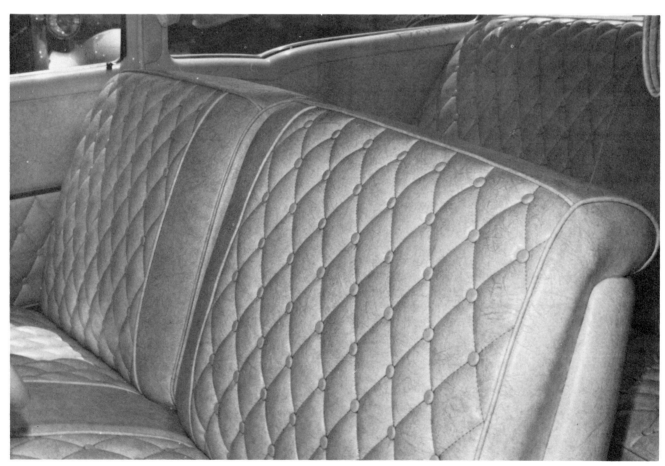

A topstitched design like this can be laid out on the cover material and sewn directly to the backing. All lines in one direction are sewn first, then the ones in the opposite direction. Buttons are added at intersecting points.

Making a tufted panel

Rather than decoration alone, more definition is usually desired in a button-tufted job. This can be achieved without sewing by cutting holes through a thick block of foam with a punch or a sharpened piece of tubing. The buttons and the cover material are then tucked down into the holes and the buttons secured to a backing. A fold is made in the cover material between each pair of buttons; the pressure of the compressed foam will maintain that fold. The foam can also be sliced part way through along the pattern lines, leaving a minimum of 1/4 inch uncut, and the cover material tucked into the slit.

A fairly rigid backing such as Masonite or 3/16 inch plywood should be used as the base for button-tufted panels constructed this way. Entire door, quarter or kick panels or smaller sections to be inserted in panels can be made up. Button-tufted seats can also be made this way directly on a wooden frame or platform. For a headliner, or seat for that matter, a heavy but pliable material such as canvas would be preferable for a backing.

On the backing, mark the center line in both directions. Using the center of the panel as indicated by the intersection of these lines as a reference point, lay out the tuft design you've worked out on your plan or pattern. Draw in the lines that will form the design

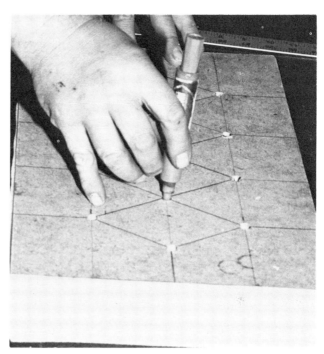

Transfer this pattern to a block of foam by tracing through holes with a marker. Thickness of the foam will be determined by how puffy you want the tufts to be. The one shown is two inches thick, made by gluing together two one-inch pieces.

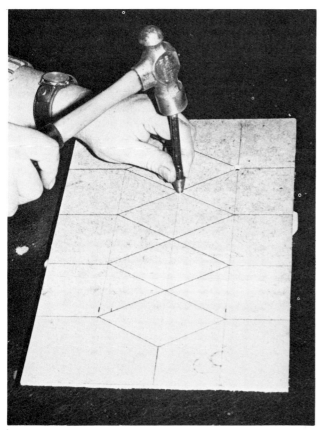

To make diamond tufts, draw the pattern onto a stiff board such as Masonite or plywood. The center line should also be drawn in both directions (the vertical one is not drawn in this picture). Punch a 3/8 inch hole at each point where lines intersect.

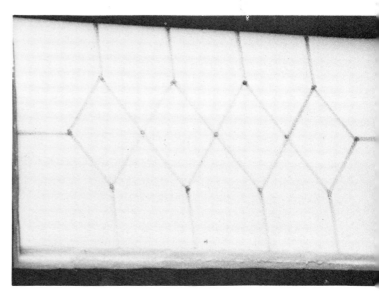

Draw the diamond pattern onto the foam.

73

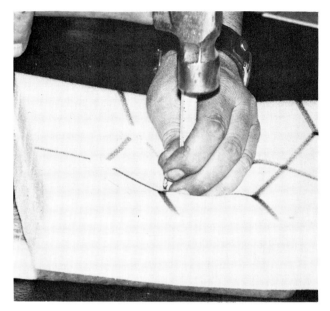

Punch button holes in the foam slightly larger than the button size. If the finished button will be ⁵⁄₈ inch, holes should be ³⁄₄ inch and so on. A sharpened piece of tubing will make the holes if you don't have a punch.

and mark the button locations wherever the lines cross.

If the backing is wood, punch or drill a hole ¹⁄₄ inch to ³⁄₈ inch in size at each button point. Now lay the backing over the sheet or block of foam padding and with a marker, mark the button points onto the foam. If the backing is canvas, you may pierce the canvas with an awl and make the mark with a ballpoint or

felt-tip pen. Remove the backing and "connect the dots" to put the pattern onto the foam.

Punch holes in the foam for the buttons. They should be slightly larger than the buttons to be inserted. For example, if the finished button is ⁵⁄₈ inch in diameter, make the hole ³⁄₄ inch. A sharpened piece of tubing will handle the job if you don't have a punch.

A word here regarding the cover material. Stick to something plain for this type of button-tufting work. Stripes or patterns are difficult to line up and keep going in the same direction, so it's hard to make the job look good.

A choice is available when it comes to buttons. For a side panel job particularly, the prong-type button is the easiest to install. Simply push it through the material and the hole in the foam until the head contacts the backing and the prongs extend through the hole in the backing. Then bend the prongs over on the back.

The other type of button has an eyelet on the back. Twine is run through the eyelet and inserted through the foam and backing and secured on the back side. Old coat buttons from a thrift store work well for this. The eyelet button has the advantage that it can be pulled down to different depths, and it does not have to be inserted all the way to the backing.

Determining material requirements

Assuming that more than an inch of padding is going to be employed for this procedure—two inches of padding is normal for this type of job—additional material will be required to give the tufts the desired fullness. To estimate material requirements, lay out one tuft on a small piece of the type of cover fabric to be

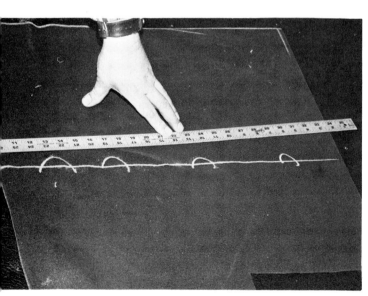

Mark the center lines in both directions on the back of the cover material. Allow plenty on all sides.

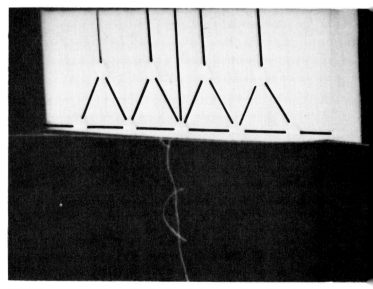

Fold the cover back on the horizontal center line. Line it up with the horizontal center line on the foam, which is placed (glued if you wish) on the panel board, and align the vertical center lines.

used. Add 1½ inches in each direction, which should be close to the amount required. Thus, if the tuft is to be four inches wide and 5½ inches high, it would be marked on the fabric 5½ wide and seven inches high.

Insert buttons at the four corners. The resulting tuft should be smooth and even. If it is loose or wrinkled, slightly less allowance should be made for fullness. If a crease forms across the tuft, it is too tight and slightly more allowance is required. Make adjustments by adding or subtracting ¼ inch at a time and refitting the trial tuft until it is as desired. With the trial piece of cover again removed and spread flat, the measurements between the button locations thus determined, horizontally and vertically, are those which will determine the size of the cover piece and the tuft layout on it.

To figure the cover measurements in each direction, multiply the distance between buttons times the number of buttons minus one, then add the distance to each outside edge and you have the overall dimensions of the cover material. As always, it's best to allow a little extra besides. The pattern you draw onto the cover material must reflect these button-to-button measurements, whereas the pattern on the backing material will be that of the actual finished tuft size.

Constructing a tufted panel

Now you should have your panel board with the tuft design marked and holes punched at the button locations, a foam pad done the same way, the cover with the design marked on it (including the extra measure for fullness) and a batch of buttons.

Begin tufting in the center of what will be the back or bottom of the piece. Insert a button and secure

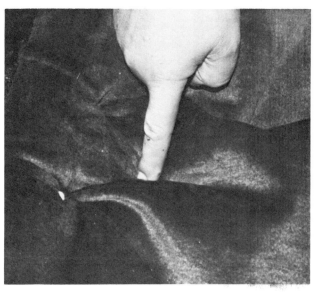

Push the material into the next hole, working up and out from the starting point. Position material before inserting the button. For the inexperienced, a more even layout will be assured if the button layout—including allowance for fullness—is drawn onto the front of the cover and buttons inserted at the indicated locations.

it on the back side of the board. Working outward to the left and right, place the first row of buttons. If the design is to be a square or rectangle, fold a pleat into the material between buttons as each button is inserted. Face the pleat downward or toward the front of the piece.

Go to the second row and again working from the center out, insert each button, forming a pleat be-

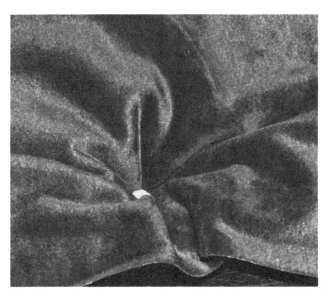

Begin inserting buttons at what will be the bottom middle of the panel and work up and out to both sides. Push button through the cover material and into the hole until it contacts the board and the prongs pass through to the back side.

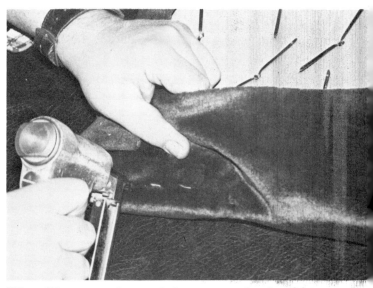

When all buttons are in, stretch the cover over the edge of the board and staple on the back side.

75

tween it and the adjacent buttons in the first row. In a diamond pattern you'll be folding in two diagonal pleats—both turned down or toward the front—for each new button you put in. For a square or rectangle design you'll make a pleat between the button being inserted and the one behind it as well as the one to the left or right. Vertical pleats in a rectangular design should face toward the outside.

As you go, or after the tufting is completed, pleats can be adjusted to a certain degree to give them the desired appearance. A length of wooden dowel can be sanded smooth on the end to serve as a probe to help adjust the pleats, either on the outside or between the cover and the foam.

When tufting on the panel is complete, pleats can be formed running vertically or horizontally to the edge of the cover, pulled around the edge and stapled to the back of the panel board. Staple each pleat location first to be sure it is properly positioned. Then staple around the entire border at 1/2 inch to one inch intervals, and trim the excess material 1/4 inch from the staple line.

A door or side panel thus constructed is now ready to install. If it's a smaller panel, it is ready to be combined with whatever other components are to be included in the design.

A tufted panel to be used for a seat covering, headliner or for attachment to other upholstered components should be constructed on a piece of canvas or burlap backing rather than panel board. It can be easily sewn together with the other pieces and won't be too rigid to sit on.

Tufting a seat platform

Board-backed tufted cushions can be used on seats. For the desired cushioning, two inches of medium to high-density foam is suggested for the back; two to four inches is recommended for the seat along with another two-inch layer between the tufted cover and the seat frame.

Reproduction fiberglass bodies that have become widely popular as the basis of street rods, customs and sports cars often require the construction of a plywood seat platform. This is usually cut to shape from 1/2 inch plywood.

For a curved seat back such as in a roadster or touring car, a template or pattern of the area to be covered is made from heavy paper or cardboard and transferred to a piece of 3/16 inch plywood. By applying steam or soaking in a hot tub, the plywood can be bent to the right contours.

The tuft design is then laid out on the plywood, the button locations marked and a 1/4 inch hole drilled at each point. The design is then transferred to a two-inch sheet of foam and the cover material laid out as described previously. Proceed with the tufting directly onto the plywood back. The material is stretched over the edges of the board and stapled.

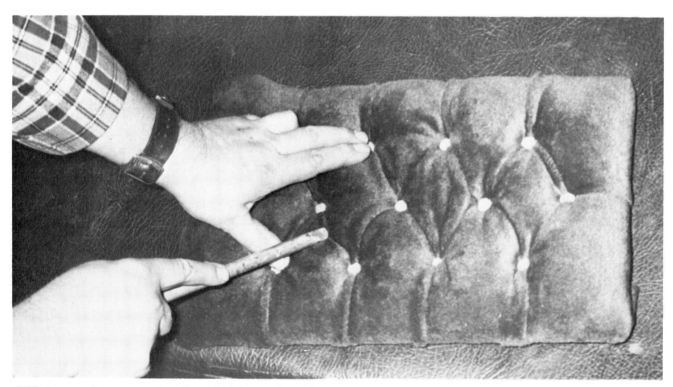

Folds between buttons can be adjusted with a probe made from a smooth wooden dowel.

In a roadster or touring car, it may be that the tufting job will be finished after the seatback is installed in the car. In this case, extra padding is often inserted to build up the roll at the top of the backrest, then the cover is pulled over and stapled to a tack strip on the outside of the body. A decorative or finishing strip is then installed to hide the staples.

The tufted seat cushion is constructed as described above; again, a canvas or burlap backing is preferable to Masonite or plywood for comfort's sake. Additional foam padding is cut to shape and glued to the plywood seat platform. The tufted cushion is then glued on top of the foam. It is finished off as above, with the covering being stretched over and stapled to the bottom of the plywood platform.

Remember to staple in the center first and work outward. If pleats are to continue around the edge, fold them into the material first and staple them into the correct position in line with the buttons. When the cover is correctly aligned with a few staples, go back and staple the edge at 1/2 inch intervals. Trim the material 1/4 inch from the staple line.

Sewn tufts

Pleats sewn into the cover between buttons, along with padding slit to allow the cover to pull down, will create distinct tufts with less fabric and eliminate the need to hand form each pleat. Sewn tufts are usually made with a thinner layer of padding, one-inch thick or so.

To incorporate 1/4 inch pleats between buttons, adjust the measurements of the layout you draw onto the back of the cover material by 1/2 inch per button from the pattern put onto the foam and backing.

Fold the cover, back side out, on each pattern line and sew 1/4 inch inside the fold. Some upholsterers sew in an arc between each pair of buttons, which creates more of a pocket for the button. First sew all the pleats in one direction, that is, parallel with each other. Then go back and sew the pleats across in the opposite direction.

Punch holes for the buttons just beside each intersection. Be consistent in putting the holes in the same position relative to the seam, but be careful not to cut the thread. Now the cover and buttons can be attached to the foam and backing as before.

Tufts without buttons

It's possible to achieve the button-tufted effect without the buttons. In this case, tucks are taken in the material and pulled down where the buttons would be.

The cover is prepared as described above for sewn tufts. Instead of sewing the pleats up to the button points, about 1/4 inch is left at each button point. Then a piece of twine is inserted at these points and tied to the fabric. The twine is then pulled through the foam and backing and secured to the backing in the same way a button would be. Thus a tuck is pulled into the cover and secured in place of a button.

Topstitching adds definition to a diamond design when deeper tufts aren't required. This design has 1/2 inch of foam backing.

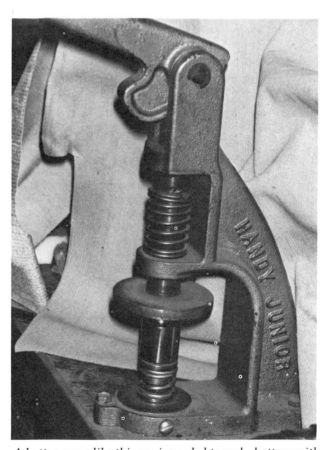

A button press like this one is needed to make buttons with your upholstery material. Ready-made buttons are available in many styles including chrome and gold, or you can take some of your material to an upholstery shop to have buttons made.

Topstitching tufts

Another method of defining a tuft design is by top-stitching through the backing. The design is drawn onto the face side of the cover and the cover placed over a sheet of 1/4 inch or 1/2 inch foam. Then the material is sewn along the lines, first all those running in one direction and then those going the opposite way.

Thicker foam can be used if slits are cut into it along the design lines to 1/4 inch from the backing cloth (not all the way through). Tuck the cover material down into the slits, pin it in place if necessary, and hold the slits open as you sew. Further information on this technique is in the roll-and-pleat section. Punch holes and add buttons as described above for sewn pleats.

Buttons

The types of buttons were mentioned briefly in Chapter 3 but need to be discussed here in a bit more depth. If you cannot get prefinished buttons suitable for your upholstery job, and don't wish to invest in a button-making machine, consider taking your buttons and a piece of material to an upholstery shop to have them made up.

The type of button for seats and heavily padded pieces has an eyelet in the back. A length of button twine is tied to it, inserted through the fabric and padding, and tied to the seat frame or secured to the backing with a wad of cotton or a large shirt or coat button to keep it from pulling through.

To tie twine to the button so it will slip as it is tightened, first put the twine around one side of the eyelet, then put both ends through the eyelet from the other side. To make an upholsterer's figure-eight knot that can be tightened to pull the buttons down to a uniform depth, take one strand of twine in each hand. Hold the left one straight. Loop the right strand under the left, then back over both, under and around both and finally through the first loop. When the left strand is pulled, the right can be slid up, pulling the button tighter. When tightened to the desired position, tie an overhand knot to hold the figure-eight knot in place.

Sew facing for the pillow to a piece of cloth-backed foam and trim, leaving 1/4 inch for attachment.

Three sections of vinyl joined together, and with a length of welt sewn to the inside edge, make up the flounce for the pillow. Sew the flounce to the edge of the facing.

Pillowbacks

A seat style that's drifted over from the furniture industry to automobiles is the pillowback or pillow cushion. As the name implies, it consists of a padded element constructed like a pillow, enclosed on three or four sides and attached to the back or cushion of the seat. Though employed mostly to heighten the luxury look, it also adds some padding and imparts somewhat of a floating feeling to the rider.

The pillowback is not easy to construct. It requires an industrial sewing machine and a lot of patience, and experience is a big plus. So if this is your first attempt at upholstering a car, you may do well to begin with something simpler, or find a good set of pillowback seats from a late-model car and trim the rest of the interior to match them.

Layout and measurement

As usual, start with a pattern. Determine the portion of the seat to be covered by the pillow; usually it will be most of the seating portion. You can put pillows

A piece of cloth sewn to the back of the pillow forms a sack into which a piece of one-inch foam is inserted. When the foam is in place, hog-ring the sack opening shut.

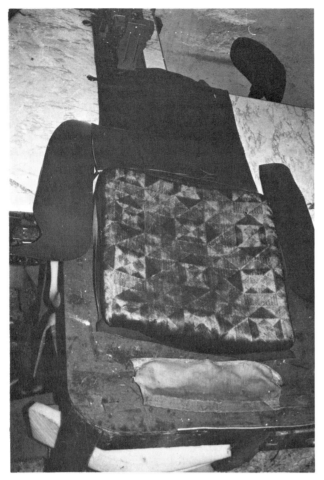

Lay out the finished pillow with individual vinyl pieces for the rest of the cover: two sides, the top, outside back and the cloth tail for attachment.

on both cushion and back or the back alone. If you don't have a pillowback seat to work from, make a full-scale model or pattern of the pillow and the rest of the seat covering and follow it in laying out the material.

The pillow itself consists of a front panel and three pieces joined together to form a partial back or rim. A thicker or more distinct pillow, if desired, requires two additional side panels and a top panel. The partial back panels are joined to the top and side bolsters of the seat covering, which is in turn joined to the back to complete the cover.

From the pattern, draw the outline of the pillow's face panel onto the upholstery material and cut it out, leaving at least a couple inches on all sides. Cut a matching piece of 1/2 inch cloth-backed foam and sew the cover material to it around the marked edge. Trim the edge 1/4 inch outside the seam.

In the same manner, trace from your pattern the pieces that will form the rim. The material may match the facing or the rest of the seat covering, or it may be a different but complementary fabric. You'll be ahead to choose the easiest material to work with, which favors a cloth over a vinyl or leather. The pillow facing is often done in a different material or color for contrast.

Cut out these pieces, sew them to 1/4 inch foam and trim just outside the seam. These three pieces are now sewn together with blindstitching. The seams will be at the upper corners of the pillow. Now sew a welt along the full length of this piece on the edge that will attach to the facing.

Determine and mark the center of the top edge of both the face and the rim, and make alignment marks at several corresponding points on both parts. With

Two cover pieces are shown joined together with welt sewn to the edge that will attach to the pillow. Sew on the back side with the two pieces being joined laid face to face and the joining edges aligned.

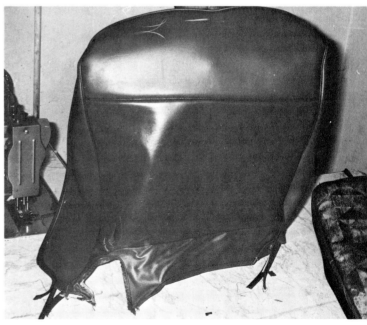

Sew the back together with welts to strengthen each seam.

the two pieces face to face, begin at the top center point and sew around in one direction, checking for equal stretching at each alignment point. After reaching the end, start at the center again and sew around the other side. Finish by cutting a piece of muslin or similar material (it won't show) the size of the pillow and sewing it to the back to form a sack to contain the foam padding for the pillow.

Set the completed pillow aside, and construct the rest of the seat cover. It consists of a top, two side bolsters and an outside back panel which form a horseshoe shape into which the pillow fits. Trace these elements onto the chosen cover material from patterns and cut them out. Depending upon the kind of seat padding under the cover, these panels may or may not require padded backing. If it is molded foam, as shown in the photos, no backing is necessary. If it is a seat built up with layers of foam, add a backing of 1/4 inch or 1/2 inch foam to give the cover a smooth finish.

Sew welting around these three joined panels on the edge that joins the back panel. Sew the top panel

Measure and mark the pillow face with chalk for installation of buttons. The job pictured is a re-covering in the original style, and the original two-pronged buttons have been saved for reinstallation. The prongs go through the foam of the pillow and secure on the back side of the sack.

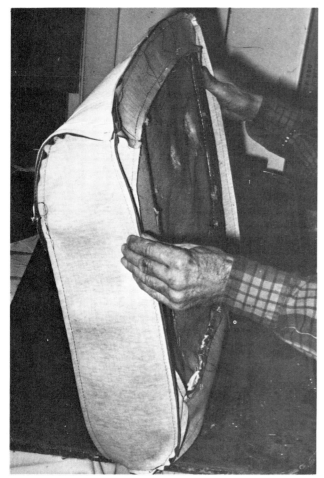

Turn the cover inside out for sewing the pillow section to it. The cover will have a horseshoe-shaped opening into which the pillow section fits.

With buttons inserted, the pillow back is ready to be installed on the seat. Taking the original cover apart and marking the individual pieces, then cutting corresponding new pieces and assembling them in the same fashion, is the only way to finish a job like this.

to the back panel, and the two bolsters to the top and the side panels to form the horseshoe. Sew welting around the free edge of this section. Both the back section and the front, or pillow, section must now be placed together face to face, or inside out. Again working from the top center, sew the sections together in one direction, then return to the center and sew the other side.

The cover is now turned right side out. Again using your pattern for the pillow face, trace the outline onto a piece of medium-firm foam one inch thick and cut it out. Insert the foam piece into the "sack" you sewed to the back of the pillow. When it is situated correctly with no folds or bulges, hog-ring the sack opening shut.

If buttons are to be used to decorate and tuft the pillow and help hold the foam in place, install them at this point. Mark the locations on the face of the pillow, double-checking the measurements. With an awl, punch holes for inserting prong-type buttons. Take precautions to avoid piercing through to the back panel. Then insert and secure the buttons. The pillow-back cover is ready to install on the seat.

Other designs

The possibilities for adding designs and decoration to your upholstery job are truly limited only by the imagination—and the availability of a sewing machine. Various effects can be created with buttons, pleats and padding, but stitching a design into a panel greatly expands the choices.

This is feasible on a home machine if you're working with a relatively lightweight fabric, but probably not with vinyl or a heavy backing material. Also, you should do a lot of practicing to develop proficiency in handling the machine before attempting new designs.

Stitched

One way of adding a design is to stitch it into the cover material directly. Make a pattern by drawing your design on paper, then transfer it to the face of the material.

Cut a piece of 1/4 inch cloth-backed foam large enough to encompass the area of the design and several inches on all sides, or to cover all or part of the panel. Apply adhesive to both surfaces and allow it to

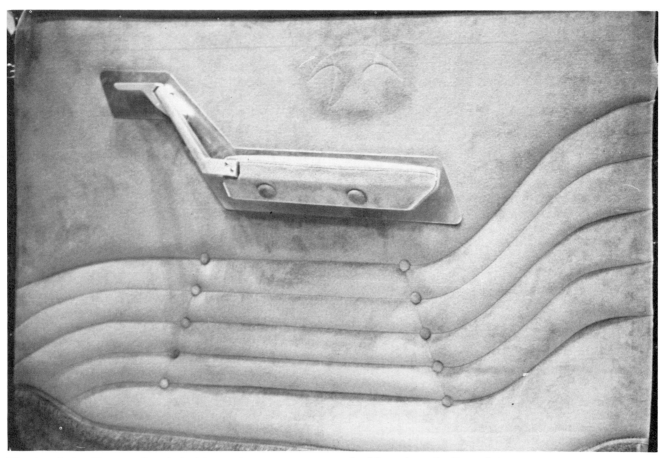

Flowing design lines can be stitched into a door panel and decorated with buttons. Topstitching with a 1/2 inch foam backing gives the lines definition. Button prongs extend through the panel board and secure on the back.

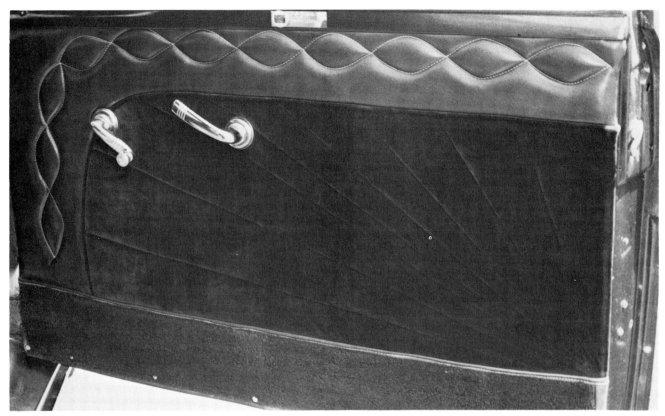

A chain design is stitched into the vinyl border of this door panel and sun rays into the velour insert. In both cases, the design is drawn onto the cover and topstitched with foam backing providing the three-dimensional definition.

The entire layout of the panel must be drawn onto the back side of the cover material. A simple design of three raised ribs is going to be put in just below the handle and window crank locations (circles) to add interest to an otherwise flat door panel.

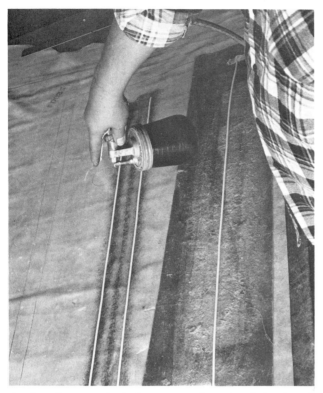

Apply adhesive to both the cover and a strip of plastic welt cord. When dried until it's tacky, glue the welt cord in place along the design lines drawn on the cover.

Glue a piece of scrap fabric over the welt cord strips. This should be a tightly woven fabric that will hold stitches securely.

become tacky. Then glue the foam to the back of the cover fabric. Sew in the design, stitching around the lines on the material. The machine will sew through the backing, and the foam will give it a sculptured look.

The same procedure can be followed without the padded backing, the stitching alone tracing the design. You'll probably want to use a contrasting color of thread in this case, but for the relief (or padded) design, either the same or a contrasting color will do, depending upon how distinct you wish the design to be.

Welt cord

A second method of putting a design into upholstery is to define the lines with welt cord. The outline will be raised from the surrounding surface by about half the thickness of the cord. Thread the same color as the cover is recommended, as lines of stitches will be parallel, and any irregularities will be more evident with a contrasting color.

If you've made a paper pattern of the panel as suggested earlier, develop your design ideas on it first.

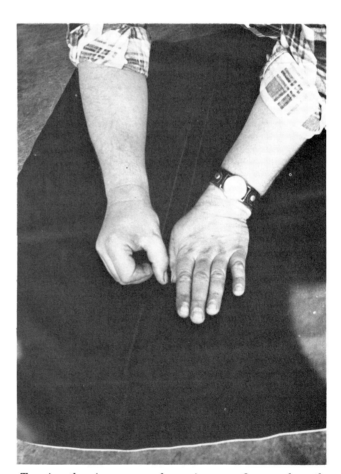

Turning the piece over and running your fingers along the ribs before the glue is set will help give sharp definition to the design.

The layout of the entire panel, including locations of hardware and division lines between sections, is then drawn in pencil or chalk onto the back side of the covering. Now glue welt cord to the material, following the lines of the design. The glue will hold the cord in place until it is sewn in. Trim the ends of the cord.

Cover this area with a piece of fabric—a discarded scrap, sheet or piece of cheesecloth will do. It should have a weave tight enough to hold the stitches, but be thin enough that its outline won't be visible through the covering. Glue the fabric in place over the welt cord.

Turn the material over, and on the front side press it tightly against the welt to make a well-defined line. Stitch tightly against the edge of the welt. Begin sewing somewhere in the middle of the design and on the bottom side, if there is a bottom, and sew all the way around, ending up where you began. Finish by sticking the "tails" of thread through to the back side and tying them. You will have no "tails" or loose ends showing on the outside, and the beginning and ending point will be in the least visible spot.

Cardboard

A third approach is similar to the previous one, but with a piece of cardboard to define the design, resulting in less distinction in the sculptured effect. Again, start by tracing or drawing the entire panel layout onto the back side of the cover, including the design you wish to emboss. Transfer the design to a

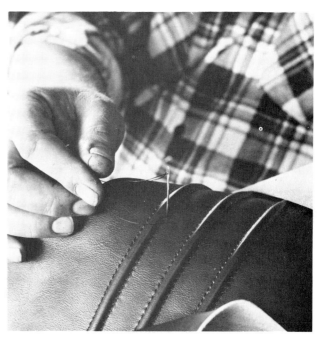

To finish off the stitching, insert the tails of thread through the eye of a needle and pull them through to the back side.

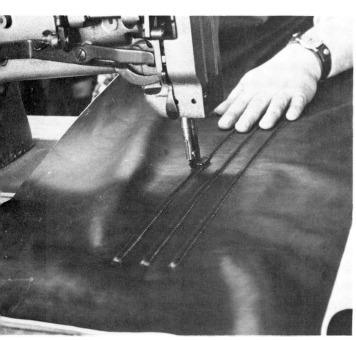

Use a sewing machine welt foot attachment to stitch around each strip of cord. Start and end near the middle to make uniform stitches all around and hide the start-stop point.

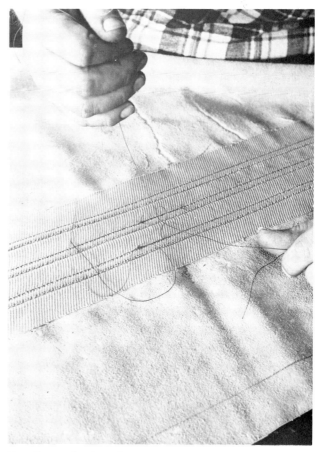

Finally, tie the thread tails off in back to prevent them from pulling loose.

Ornaments such as musical notes and figures can be attached to panels. They can be made up on cardboard or Masonite and attached with clips, thread or glue to the panels.

This music and dance theme was done by Bob McQuality on his 1950 Mercury.

Decorative and functional ornaments can be obtained from a salvage yard. The fancy door handle and surrounding housing—plus a remote mirror control from a late-model luxury car—were added to this 1955 Chevy door panel.

piece of light cardboard, or draw it directly onto the cardboard. Cut out the cardboard design, position it and glue it into place on the back of the fabric. Glue a piece of backing cloth over the cardboard as outlined above.

Turn the material over, press it tightly around the cardboard to define the outside line, then stitch around the border as instructed with welt cord.

Ornaments

Another way to individualize your interior design is to attach ornaments or figures. Human figures, musical notes, dice and other designs have been used to carry out special themes on some custom cars.

These may be made up of the regular interior fabric or something completely different. Since such ornamentation usually isn't placed where it will be subject to wear, the durability is not so much of a factor. Using the method described above (cutting the design out of cardboard) is recommended. Cover the cardboard form with fabric, wrapping it around the edges and gluing in back. The ornament can then be stitched or glued to the finished panel.

A salvage yard is a treasure trove of small trim pieces, both exterior and interior, to decorate a custom interior. Different styles of buttons and ornaments can be found on various seats and door panels. Crests, nameplates and script are easy to adapt, usually requiring only small holes to mount. The more luxurious cars may offer special courtesy lights, grab bars and armrests.

Sculpturing

A custom upholstery technique that's gained a lot of popularity in recent years is sculpturing. It involves creating a design with panels of different textures, inserting sections raised above or sunk below the surrounding surface or both. On seats, thicker padding may be cut into sections and covered so the sections remain distinct with sharp, deep channels between.

On a flat panel on which the design has been drawn in pencil or chalk, foam is cut to the required shape of the raised portions and glued into place. A sheet of 1/4 inch foam is then glued over the entire panel and shaped around the raised areas to form a base for the cover. Finally the cover is applied with a coat of adhesive and also shaped around the raised portions, then finished over the edges of the panel.

More distinct sculpturing is done with thicker foam. A high-density material will maintain the desired shape better. The foam is cut to shape and glued to the panel board. Cover material is applied over it, pulled down snugly and glued, then trimmed outside the padded area; leaving an extra inch or so will be sufficient to secure the cover to the panel board.

Insert pieces are then made up which can be of the same material or contrasting in color, fabric or texture. Thicker or thinner foam may be used, depending on the effect desired. Make up inserts on pieces of Masonite cut to shape and fitted with bolts or clips for attachment to the panel. Drill the appropriate attachment holes in the panel board.

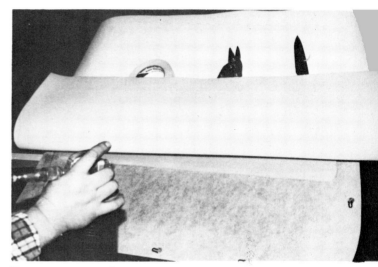

You can create sculpturing by layering foam. Cut quarter-inch high-density foam to shape and glue it to the panel board. Then glue another layer of foam over the entire panel. Shape it snugly to the contours of the first layer.

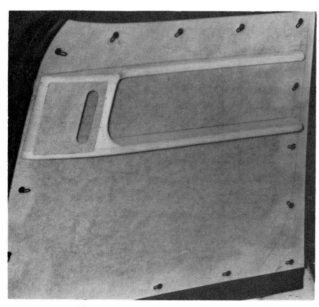

Armrests and grips for the doors of this street rod were cut out of wood, shaped and sanded smooth. They will be finished in leather.

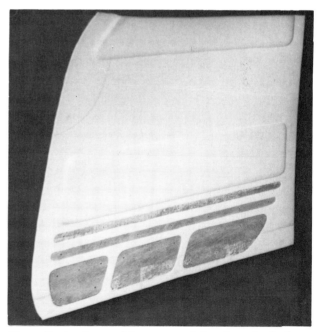

Shape the top layer of foam around the pieces in the lower layer to create the high and low effect. At the bottom of this panel, portions have been trimmed out for inserts.

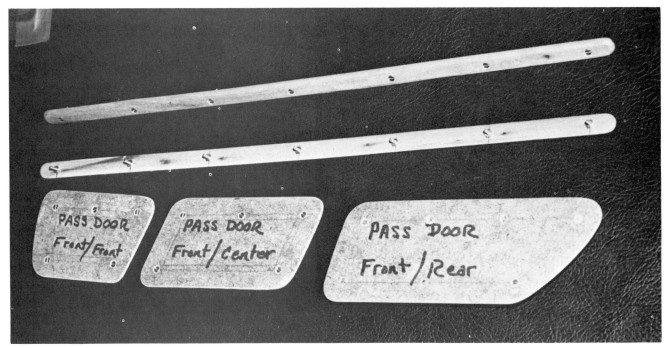

Here, insert pieces were cut and shaped from wooden molding, top, and Masonite, bottom.

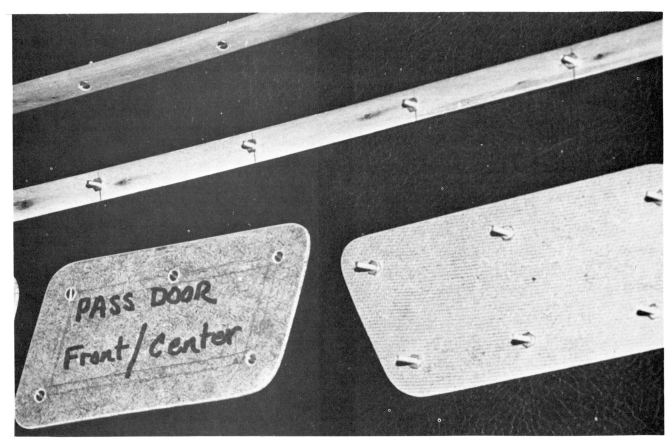

Attach quarter-inch bolts to the inserts with a set of nuts. A second set of nuts will secure them to the door panel.

The wood hand grip is padded with a layer of 1/4 inch foam, finished with a leather covering. The cover must be glued to the foam, stretched and shaped around the wood and stapled on the back side. If done carefully, heating with a hair dryer will make the vinyl more pliable and easier to stretch. A woven fabric is easier to work with than the leather.

To create sculptured seats, cut thick blocks of foam for the desired rolls. Fit the cover material over the foam and make a fold where the channel must be. Then sew a pleat along the fold. Either sew a listing strip to this pleat, or make the pleat deep enough that a stiff wire can be inserted through it. When the cover

The finished door panel is covered in leather. Horizontal strip inserts are a different color of leather, while bottom inserts are finished with carpet material. There's a relief in the panel where the door grip attaches, and gray suede is used under the grip for contrast.

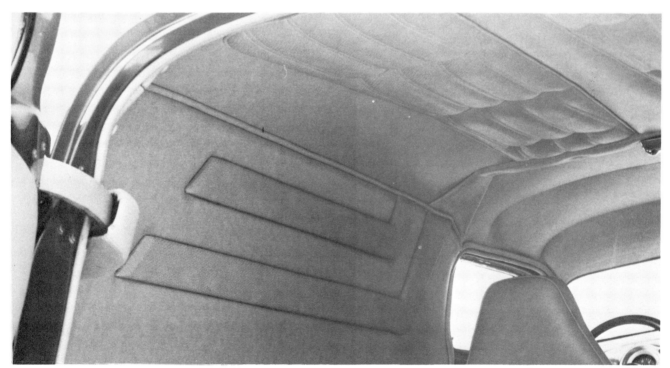

Headliner sculpturing such as this involves cutting out sections of the foam backing before installing the cover. Then

separate blocks of foam are cut to fit, covered with matching or contrasting material and inserted into the openings.

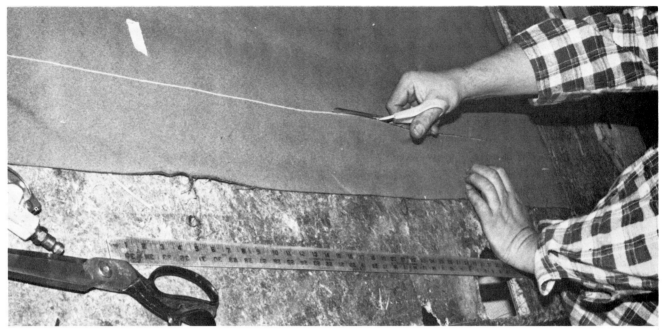

To make windlacing, cut a strip of the desired cover material about four inches wide.

Apply adhesive to the length of rubber windlace core and evenly to the back of the cover fabric. Allow it to set up until tacky. The procedure is the same for making welting, but material can be cut narrower for the smaller welt cord.

is installed over the foam padding, the wire is pulled down and secured to the framework with hog rings to hold the channel in place.

A similar result could also be achieved by constructing the sculptured seat covering on a heavy backing of canvas or burlap. It could then be done as described in the section on making rolls and pleats: the channel is sewn to the backing, a block of foam is

Fold the material over for a smooth finish on the end. Place the welt core in the center of the strip and wrap the material around it.

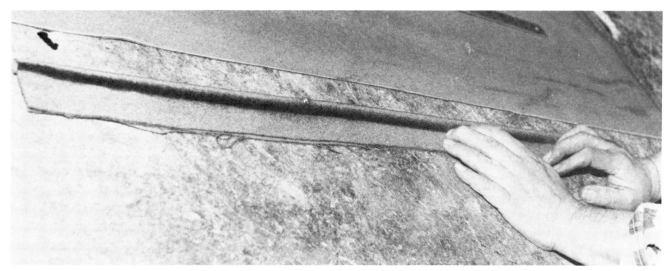

Align the edges and press the material together, taking care to press the material firmly against the core.

glued to the backing next to the seam, the cover is pulled over the foam block and the next channel sewn to the backing, and so on.

Making piping

The availability of piping or welting material in a wide range of colors and fabrics was mentioned previously. However, if none of these is suitable, or if you simply prefer to make your own, here is the procedure. White plastic welt cord, which comes in various sizes from $3/32$ inch to $5/32$ inch, is the easiest to work with.

Cut cover material in strips $1^1/2$ inches wide and as long as the material will allow; here's where you can use the long, narrow leftover edges from your other cuttings. To make longer strips, join two together by cutting the ends cleanly at a forty-five-degree angle and either sewing with a blind seam or overlapping and gluing. The junction will be barely visible.

Spray or brush trim adhesive to the back of the fabric strip, and allow it to sit until the glue becomes tacky. Then center the welt cord on the strip, carefully fold the fabric over the cord and press it firmly. Of course, if a sewing machine with a welt foot is handy, sewing may supplant the gluing process.

If a sewing machine is available, stitching with a welt foot attachment will hold the windlace cover firmly.

Trim excess material, leaving about $1/2$ inch for attachment.

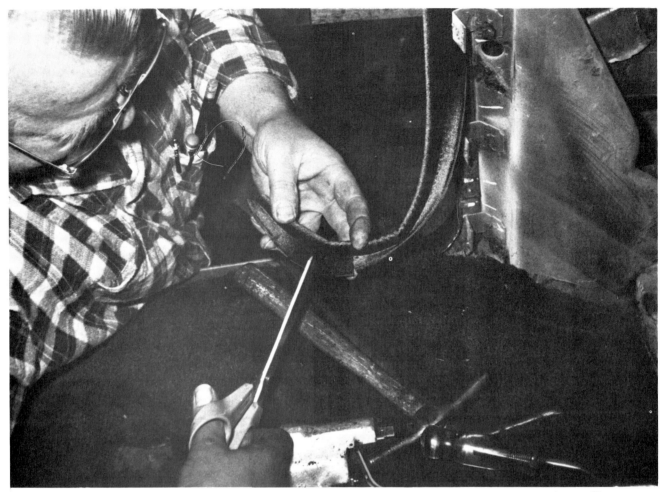

When attaching, determine where the windlace must bend around corners. Make cuts nearly through the attachment flap at about 1/2 inch intervals to allow the windlace to curve smoothly.

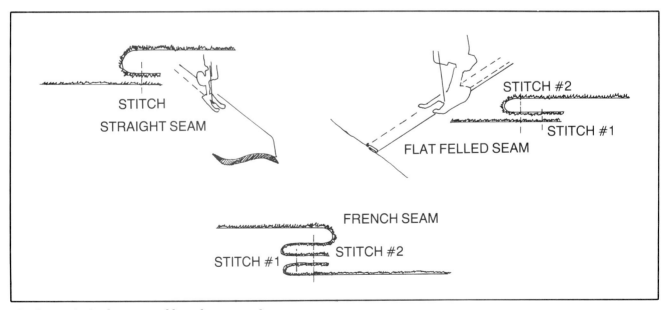

STITCH
STRAIGHT SEAM

STITCH #2
STITCH #1
FLAT FELLED SEAM

FRENCH SEAM
STITCH #1 STITCH #2

The three principal seams and how they are made.

Seams

Instruction in how to sew would require at least an entire book in itself. As I mentioned in the beginning, there are certain phases of the custom interior that are virtually impossible to accomplish without sewing, but much can be done without sewing.

When sewing is mentioned, it will be done without specific directions, with the assumption that if you are going to sew, you know how already, intend to learn or are going to farm out the sewing to someone who does know how to do it.

Before proceeding to talk about joining panels together, which can require sewing, I will briefly discuss three basic types of seams found in upholstery work so you'll be familiar with them when they're mentioned elsewhere.

Straight

The straight seam is formed by placing two pieces of material face to face and lining up the edges, then sewing parallel to and about 1/4 inch from the edge. When the two pieces are turned face out, the stitching is not visible. This type of seam has the strength of only one row of stitches, and if the material is heavy or bulky, it may not lie flat at the seam.

Flat felled

This seam is like the straight seam, but it has a second row of stitches that gives it extra strength and makes the material lie flat. The first set of stitches is made in the same manner as for the straight seam. Then one of the pieces of material is folded over, facing out, and another line of stitches is run on the outside and through the joined portion parallel with the first stitching. The drawback of this type is that one set of stitches is visible, which may not be desired.

French

The French seam is very strong and leaves no stitches visible. However, it results in four or five layers of material bunched together, which may be too bulky, especially if the fabric is heavy to begin with. It is made by placing the two pieces of material back to back and joining them with a row of stitches near the edge. Then the pieces are both turned over face to face and stitched just outside the line where the edges came together. Finally the material is again turned face out. The seam is similar to the straight seam, but with the backup strength of a second stitching.

Joining panels

While you may be working with only a single piece of material at any one time, several situations call for joining two pieces of material together. One cut of material may not cover a wide area, so a second piece may have to be added. A second color or another

Visible stitches are not distracting as long as they're perfectly straight and even.

To give the seam strength and provide a clean, even juncture line, a welt is sewn between two panels as they are being joined. Experienced trimmers can sew all three pieces together at once, as shown, but a surer approach for the amateur is to sew the welt to one piece, then join the other piece with a second sewing.

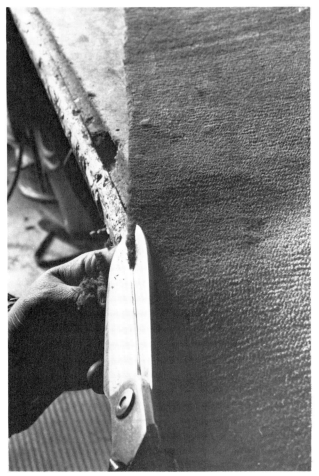

When attaching carpet to another material, trim the pile at the edge to leave a clean, straight edge.

type of material may be added for contrast. A smooth roll border is often mated to pleated or tufted panels.

Seams

Panels can nearly always be joined by hidden, straight seams with the stitching or stapling on the back side of the material. Let's say your pattern calls for a tuck-and-roll seat insert in velvet cloth with a roll of contrasting vinyl forming a border on three sides. Trace the outline of the insert from your pattern onto a second sheet of butcher or wrapping paper, and cut it out.

With the tuck-and-roll panel face down, place the pattern on it and draw around the border. Sew around the panel on this line, which is the edge of the insert panel. The excess can be trimmed an inch outside the sewn edge.

On the worktable lay out a length of the vinyl material to span the seat face. Position the paper pattern of the insert on it and draw around the edge. This is the line on which the outer roll and the insert panel will be sewn. Remove the pattern, trace another line an inch inside the first and cut out the inside section.

Now the insert panel is trimmed to size, and the outer roll is cut so the panel fits into it. They can be sewn together this way, but a welt will further define the junction and make a smoother seam. Sew a strip of welting to the border panel along the line drawn on the material for the seam.

Now place the sewing allowances of the insert and border material face to face with the welt between, and line up the edges and center points, which should be marked on both. Sew them together, stitching snugly against the welt cord. Begin at the center

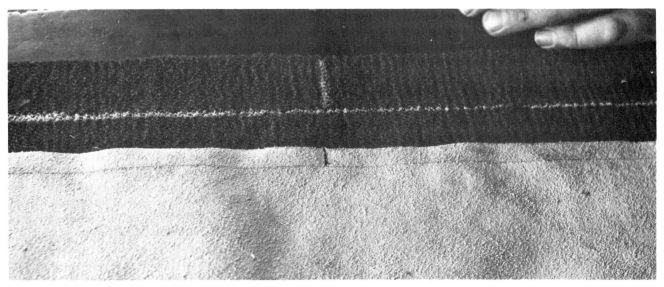

Mark the sewing line on both carpet and upholstery fabric, and mark the center line as measured from side to side. Because different types of fabric, leather, vinyl and carpet ma- *terial stretch at different rates, sew from the center out in both directions.*

and sew to one side, then return to the center and sew to the other side.

A similar procedure may be followed to make up the covering for door and side panels. It's also possible to attach the separate elements of the design to the panel individually. For example, mark the shape and size of the tuck-and-roll panel, but retain allowances for attachment on all sides. After marking its position on the panel board, apply adhesive and carefully glue the panel into place. Pull the edges that wrap around the edge of the panel and secure them on the back by stapling.

Line up a strip of welt fabric with its attachment flap and staple it into position along the line marking the edge of the tuck-and-roll design. Then place the second panel or piece of material face to face with the first and line up the edges. Put a strip of light cardboard about 1/4 inch wide across the fabric, snugged up against the welt cord, to form an even edge and a better bite for the staples. Staple from the center out

to the sides in both directions along the middle of the cardboard strip.

If desired, padding or backing may be glued to the panel board. The second piece of material is then pulled over, turned face out and secured over the edges of the panel board as was done with the tuck-and-roll panel.

Carpet trim

A popular and practical procedure in modern interiors is to attach a strip of carpeting matching that on the floor to the bottoms of the door panels. This provides a variance in texture, and color also, if you choose. The carpeting is also protective; it is better able than upholstery fabric to withstand abuse from scuffing, and it does not show mud and dirt so readily.

When attaching carpeting to another material, first trim the pile from the edge with a pair of shears; if available, an old electric hair clipper works fine, too.

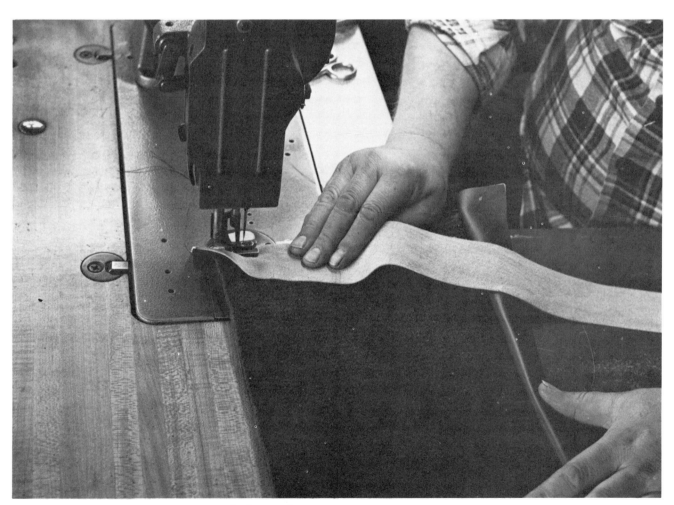

Attach the edging material to the carpet by laying the two pieces face to face, lining up the edges and sewing 1/4 inch from the edge.

Three decorative ribs are being added to this door panel, using carpet as filler. The lines were drawn onto the vinyl material, then a line of stitching was run along the chalk lines. Again, sew out in both directions from the middle.

The resulting well-defined line is easier to follow and prevents the carpet's pile from being sewn down and leaving an irregular edge.

To form an edging for the carpet, place a strip of fabric or vinyl face to face with the carpet strip, making sure the edges are even. Mark the center line of both, as the two materials will not stretch at the same rate. Sew together 1/4 inch from the edge from the center out in both directions. Attach edging to the bottom and sides of the carpet strip, and position it on the panel board. Then pull the edging over the edge of the panel board and glue or staple it in place to form a neat, firm, finished edge.

Carpeting may also serve as "filler" to add some character lines to the fabric part of the panel. The fabric is laid face down on the carpet, with the edge an inch or two in from the edge of the carpeting. Align and sew across 1/2 inch in from the edge of the fabric. Apply adhesive to the back of the fabric and front of the carpet, then turn the fabric face out, pulling it over the carpet and pressing it down firmly. Draw guidelines on the fabric with chalk and sew along the line. The pile of the carpet will fill between the stitches to give the lines definition.

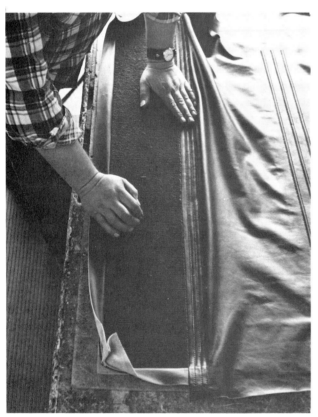

With the decorative ribs sewn in and the carpet panel joined at the bottom with vinyl edging to attach to the panel board, the finished cover is tested for fit on the panel board before attachment.

Chapter Five

Headliner upholstery

The ceiling of your interior, the headliner, may be the element least noticed by the casual observer but it's most important to the driver and passengers. A custom interior isn't complete without a nice head-liner coordinated with the rest in color, material and style.

The headliner doesn't have to be elaborate; it's not as if anyone sitting in the car looks up at it all the

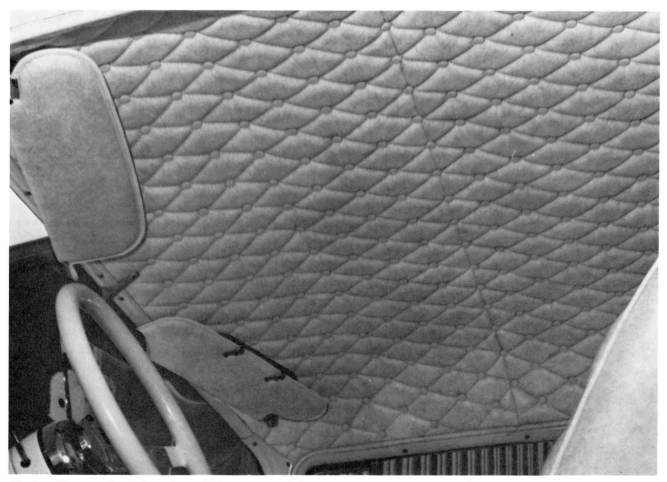

The headliner can be plain or fancy. This owner carried an elaborate button-tufted-vinyl theme through from the seats to include the headliner.

time. On the other hand, it offers the largest single expanse of material in the interior and can be used as a highlight or focal point of the interior design. One custom car following a theme of 1950s music has a headliner depicting the front of a vintage jukebox in different colors of vinyl, complete with moving colored lights.

Any of the design elements discussed in Chapter 4 can be incorporated into the headliner—buttons, diamond or square patterns, pleated panels and other designs—or it can be done simply, in plain fabric or vinyl. You may want to consider an overhead console, popularized in street rods and custom trucks, for some of the controls and radio or stereo equipment.

Fortunately for the home handyman, several companies offer ready-made headliners for most US and some foreign car models from 1928 to the present. Some of these are listed in the Appendix. They're available in original materials as well as custom flat and napped fabrics, vinyl and suede. If one of these off-the-shelf liners will suit your design, you'll save the work of making up a new one.

If you're rebuilding an old car or one that's been abused by the elements, you may not have a headliner left to remove; otherwise, there should be enough to at least be helpful in making patterns.

Removal

Remove all trim and window moldings that cover the edges of the headliner. The rear package shelf may hide the liner's edge on some cars, so it must come out, too. Remove all hardware such as dome lights and sun visors, but keep the mounting screws handy. If not done already, it's advisable to remove the seats to make room to move around the interior and provide access to the headliner attachment points.

Notice how the headliner attaches around the edges. Depending on the age of the car, it will probably be tacked or stapled to the wooden framework or a tack strip on the edge of the top. Some headliners are glued around the window openings, and others inserted into a slot. Take the headlining loose around the edges, being careful not to damage the tack strip or other parts that must be reused. A deep notch filed or ground into the blade of an old screwdriver makes a fine tool for removing tacks.

Unless the car is old with the headliner tacked to wooden strips, it will probably be hung from steel bows by means of fabric sheaths, called listing strips, sewn to the headliner at each seam. If mounting positions of the bows are not obvious, mark them, and number the bows with pieces of masking tape so

Notice how the headliner is attached. This Ford headliner is stapled across the front and tacked on the sides. Try to remove tacks and staples carefully to avoid damaging the tack strip, which is attached to the body. If the tack strip is damaged to the point of being unusable, however, new material is available.

Headliner edges are hidden by window moldings. Removing them will reveal how the liner is attached. Chevy headliner is glued and stapled into the rear window openings.

Headliner bows fit into holes along the edge of the top. Twist them forward or back when removing or installing them.

Number the bows to keep them in order, and note whether bows were in the top or bottom holes.

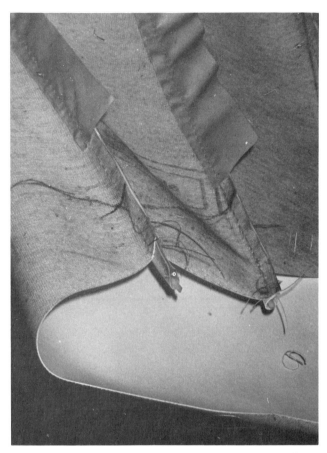

When constructing a new headliner, split the old headliner into individual sections or panels which serve as patterns for laying out and cutting new material. Sew piping to one section of headliner first, then sew the next section to the first and so on. Sew listing strips on after all sections are joined together.

Before splitting the old headliner into sections to use for patterns, number each section from front to rear.

they'll go back into the same spots. Remove the bows and headliner from the car, and remove the bows from the listing strips. Now go back and put the screws from the dome light and sun visors back into their holes to facilitate locating the holes after the new liner is in.

Inspect the bows and other hardware, and clean, refinish or replace any of it, if necessary. Rusty bows are responsible for staining headliners on some cars. If there is evidence of rust, sand and refinish them with a rust-preventive spray paint.

Construction

If a suitable ready-made headliner has been obtained, compare it with the old one to be sure it's going to fit correctly. Then proceed to installation.

Bows and listing strips

To construct a new headliner, start by taking the old one apart at the seams, numbering the panels from front to rear and stacking them in order. Lay out

Number each headliner section, and mark the side-to-side center line.

100

the headliner material face down on the worktable, lay the old headliner panels on it and draw around them. You may wish to work with two or three panels at a time, arranging them to make the best use of the material. Mark the sewing lines on the new panels, and number each as you did the old. Then cut out and stack them in order.

Custom owners often prefer to highlight the headliner with piping, either with a matching or a contrasting color, at the seams. If it is to be included, sew the piping to the first panel, then line up and sew the second panel to the first with another seam, and so on from front to rear.

Listing strips are sewn on after all the headliner panels are joined. The listing strip is merely a narrow piece of material folded to form an envelope or sheath about an inch wide for the bow to slip through. Premade cotton listing strips may be obtained, or you can make your own by cutting a strip of cotton or other material two inches wide and folding it in half lengthwise. It would be advisable to press the fold in with a steam iron to make attachment easier.

Listing strips are sewn to the headliner at each seam. Positioning them on the side of the seam toward the rear of the car makes the headliner hang better. If a welt has been included, each headliner seam will be sewn three times, providing extra strength and longevity.

Molded headliner

Rather than bows and listing strips, the headliners of some late-model cars consist of a one-piece light fabric covering cemented to a panel molded to conform to the shape of the car roof. (Some cars had a composition board lining with no fabric cover at all.) This makes a nice installation, but in humid climates the adhesive has a tendency to let go after a few years and the cover comes tumbling down.

If you face this situation, here's a way to deal with it. Remove the old fabric from the molded shell and trace around it onto a new piece of headliner material. Cut out the new liner. On the molded panel, work out a pattern of buttons that will keep the new liner up in its place while adding decoration, too. Punch or drill holes in the molded panel for prong-type buttons.

Position the new liner evenly on the panel, then fold half of the fabric back over the other half. Apply trim adhesive to the back of the fabric and to the panel, and allow it to set up until tacky. Then carefully pull the cover over and smooth into place from the middle out. (It's handy to have a second pair of hands to hold the fabric up while you press it into place a lit-

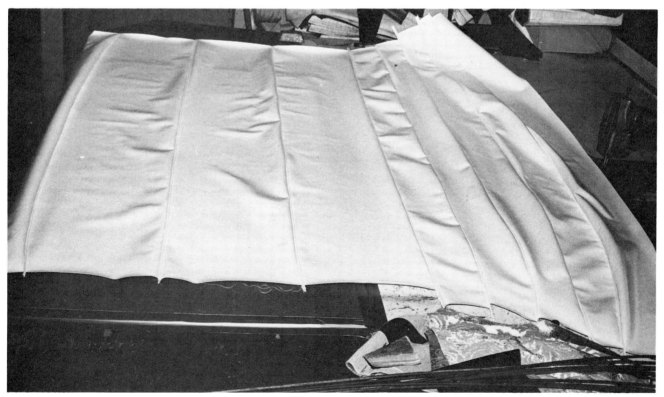

With all sections correctly sewn together with piping and listings in place, the headliner is complete and ready to install. Don't worry about trimming the edges until later

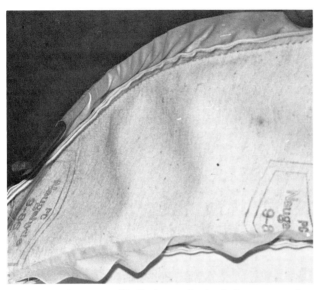

Bows must be inserted in listing strips in their proper order. If they show signs of rust, clean them so the new liner won't be stained.

tle at a time.) Repeat the procedure with the other half of the cover. Locate the holes by inserting an awl through them from the back side of the panel and insert buttons and secure the prongs on the back side. The new headliner is then ready to install.

Installation

Before tackling your headliner installation, determine whether new insulation is needed. Install that first with trim adhesive to the inside of the top. Insulation doesn't have to extend all the way to the edges.

Slide the support bows into the headliner listing strips in the proper order, front to rear, and be sure they are centered. The listing strips may be too long; trim them back about two inches from the ends of the bows so the liner can pull all the way to the side without wrinkling.

Install the rear bow first; it may have a special means of attachment. Then install the others, working toward the front. Pull the headliner snug front to

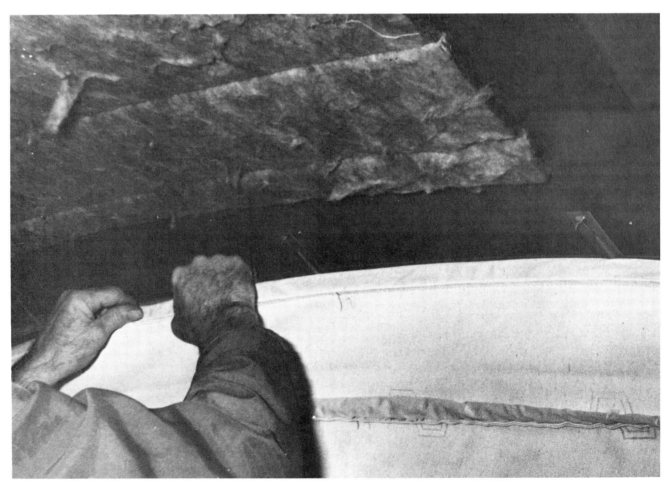

Begin at the rear of the car to install bows. This Ford has special clips to hold the back bow.

rear and side to side, work out all the wrinkles and make sure it's fitting properly.

Apply a coat of trim adhesive to the tack strip or attachment strip at the back of the top and while it's wet, pull the headliner over the strip and press it down briefly, then remove. This move will leave a line of adhesive on the back of the headliner to indicate where it attaches. Apply some more adhesive to that strip, then let both surfaces dry for a few minutes to allow the glue to become tacky.

When it has set sufficiently, pull the headliner over the tack strip and press it in place. Set the middle first, then work out toward the edges, stretching the liner both to the back and to the side as you go. After the back has had time to dry so it's not likely to pull loose, go to the front and follow the same procedure. After gluing, start at the back again and staple at one-inch intervals from the center out in each direction. Do the same in front and alternate from back to front, stapling a few inches at a time, until the front and rear are secured.

Next go to the middle of one side, pull the liner tight and staple at the seam, lining it up directly beneath the bow. Then staple the seam on either side of the first. Go to the other side of the car and do the same

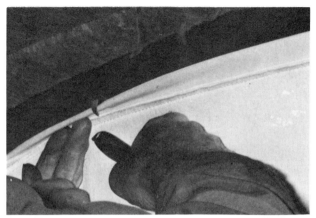

The prong of the clip must be bent over to grip the bow.

thing. Alternate sides, working from the center toward both ends. After the seams have been stapled and wrinkles have been worked out, go back and staple at about 1/2 inch intervals to make a secure attachment all the way around.

All headlining materials have a tendency to stretch, which can result in sags and wrinkles a few

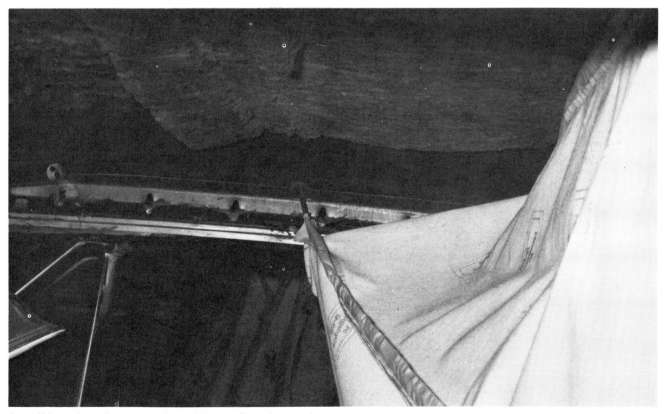

Install bows in order, rear to front. Place ends in their sockets and pivot the bow, back to front, until it is in a vertical position against the roof.

103

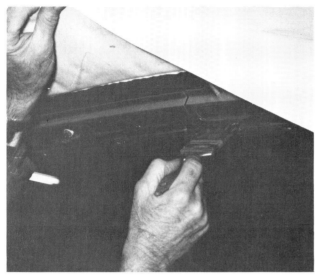

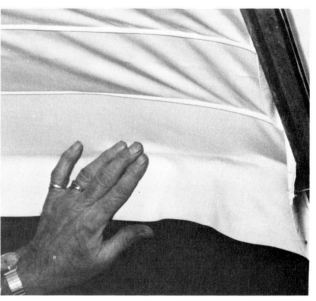

After positioning the liner and working out wrinkles, apply trim adhesive to the rear attachment strip. When the liner is pressed against the strip, then pulled away, a little glue will mark the contact point. Apply glue to the liner along this line where it contacts the attachment strip on the body.

When the adhesive becomes tacky, stretch and press the headliner into place, working from the center out toward the edges.

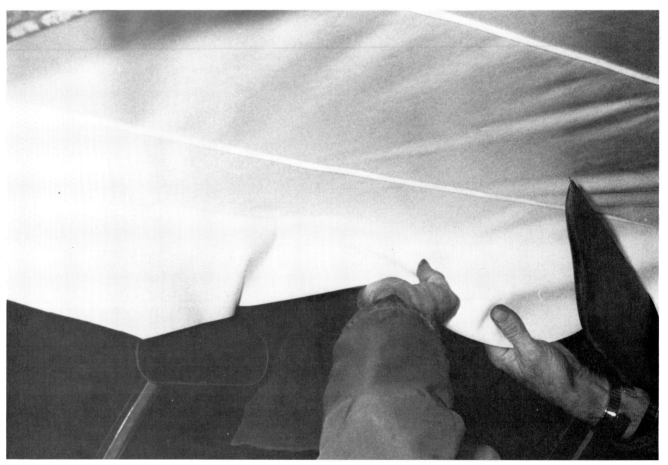

Follow the same procedure to glue the liner at the front. Stretch the liner tightly, pulling out any wrinkles from front to back. The headliner will slacken with time, so it must be applied tightly.

days or weeks after installation. It's imperative that the liner be stretched taut when it is put in so it won't sag noticeably when it begins to relax. Alternating from side to side and tacking the lining in place first is important. Going back to do the finish stapling gives you a second opportunity to pull the lining tight, even if it means replacing the original staples after additional slack has been taken out.

There may still be a few wrinkles, especially in corners, in spite of your best efforts. Even experienced trimmers don't always get them all out. That's why they keep a steamer around. Applying steam to a woven fabric headliner or heat to vinyl helps tighten it enough to remove the wrinkles.

To accomplish this in your home shop, use an electric hair dryer, but be very careful not to get it too close to the material or hold it too long in place. For woven fabric, a spray bottle can dampen a small area, which is then heated and dried with the hair dryer.

When attachment of the headliner is complete, trim the edges with scissors or a razor blade so the trim and moldings will hide them entirely. Locate the

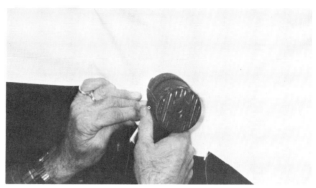

Heating a vinyl liner carefully with a hair dryer will make it pliable and easier to work into position.

screws which were inserted to mark the positions of the dome light, sun visors and other hardware. With a razor blade, make a small slit in the liner over each screw. Then remove the screws and reinstall the hardware piece. Finally, reinstall the window and side moldings to complete the job.

Stretch each seam into position initially and staple or tack at the edge. Follow by stapling solidly, working from the middle toward the front and rear and alternating from side to side. Once secured in place, the headliner can be trimmed and the window moldings reinstalled to cover the edges.

Chapter Six

Upholstering door and quarter panels

Since they are basically flat pieces, door and side panels are the easiest places for a novice to test his or her interior renovation skills. Also, they can be upholstered without a sewing machine, so the work can all be done at home. Experience gained from covering door and side panels will help you decide how much of the rest of the job to tackle yourself.

Removal

Most door panels are secured with a combination of two or more means. First, the door handles and window cranks are mounted to their respective mechanisms and the armrests to the steel inner skin in such a way as to help hold the upholstered panel in place. You must determine how each of these items is attached. The handles may be removed by taking out

straight, Phillips-head or Allen-head bolts. If no bolt head is visible, push in on the panel next to the handle and see what type of clip secures it to the shaft from behind. (Spring clips can usually be removed with a hook bent into a piece of stiff wire, or by a hooked tool, if available. A few installations require a special tool, which body shops and trim shops have, to remove the keepers.) Then slip the handles off their shafts, taking care to keep track of all the springs, clips and other hardware.

Armrests are usually secured with a pair of Phillips-head screws which tap into the steel door

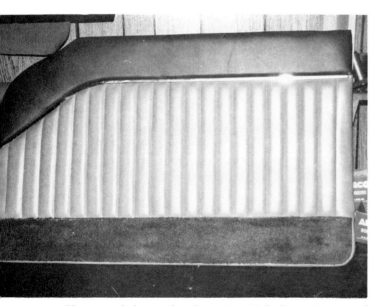

If a pressed pleat rather than a topstitched insert were used, this standard door panel could be reupholstered without any sewing.

For a shortcut, Valley Auto Accessories has molded and upholstered door panels and accessories for several popular street rod models.

skin. Other hardware and trim, such as remote mirror controls, power window controls and metal brightwork, usually is attached to the upholstered panel, not to the door skin, and doesn't have to come off in order for you to remove the panel. But you will probably have to unscrew and remove the door lock knob.

There will also be some method of attachment around the sides and bottom. Remove any visible chrome trim screws. More likely, or in addition, there are spring clips attached to the panel and secured in holes in the metal skin. Carefully insert a putty knife or screwdriver between the panel and the door skin, then slide it along until it encounters one of the clips. Work it free by twisting or carefully pulling outward on the tool. Then proceed to the next fastener and repeat the process around the edge of the panel until all clips are loose from the door.

In the 1950s, Chevrolet used a metal strip around the perimeter of the panel with nails which inserted into slots in the door skin. These are difficult to remove without breaking, but if you are trying to save them, make a removal tool by grinding a deep notch

Most door panels and some quarter panels are held on with spring clips like these. If the panel is to be reused, be very careful removing it from the car to avoid damaging the holes into which the clips are inserted.

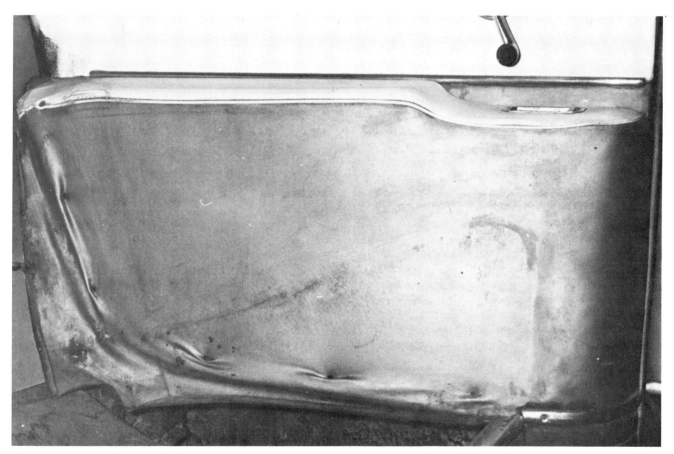

Ford quarter panels are nailed to a tack strip around the edge, with screws at the front corner. The fiberboard panel above the armrest is attached to the metal armrest section *with screws that will be visible when the entire panel is removed.*

Chevrolet door panels in the fifties employed a metal strip on the edge of the panel board with nails that insert into holes in the door skin.

into the blade of an old screwdriver. Slide the notch over the nail and carefully work it loose.

With the panel mostly loose, determine how the top is secured. On newer models it is curved over and slips into the window channel, and must be gently lifted upward until it clears the channel. On older models, the garnish molding around the window must come off by removing the Phillips screws. Then the top of the trim panel is free. There may also be clips holding the panel in the middle, requiring that the panel be slid upward to be freed.

Rear quarter panels are secured by similar means. Remove the window cranks and window framework, and remove the back seat for access to the panels. Then you should be able to see what additional fasteners must be removed. It will probably be a combination of screws and spring clips, but there may be a tack strip, hidden by the windlacing, to which the upholstered panel attaches. Take your time removing the staples or tacks so the strip isn't damaged.

Once the panel is off, remove any hardware or trim that is attached to it. Inspect the panel board to see if it is reusable. Often moisture causes it to warp or partially rot away, so chances are you will need to

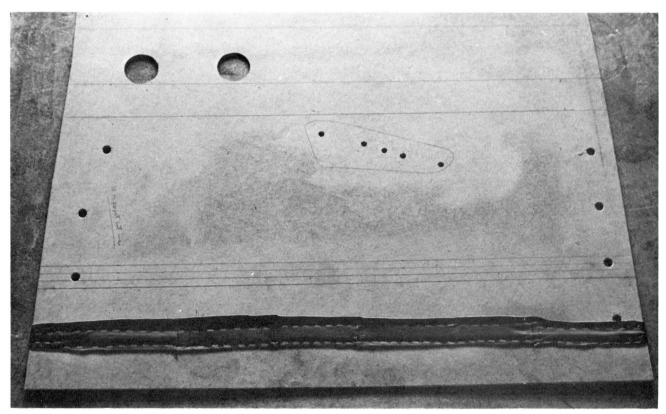

Some trimmers prefer the stiffer Masonite versus the flimsiness of panel board. Here an extra strip is attached with scrap vinyl to extend the depth or allow the board to better fit the curvature of the door. The entire design of the panel is drawn onto the panel board, and holes have been cut out for attachment of the armrest, door and window crank handles, and spring clips.

Trace the shape of the old panel onto new panel board along with window crank and trim attachment holes.

start with new board. Keep the old in one piece, however, as a pattern for the new.

Most cars have a sheet of heavy plastic or paper secured to the metal skin, with an adhesive as a seal against dust and moisture. If it is in good enough shape to reuse, leave it in place or remove it carefully. If it is not reusable, take it off as intact as possible, and keep it as a pattern for a new one.

Construction

Upholstery supply firms carry panel board for making new door and side panels. The normal thirty-two-inch by forty-eight-inch size is large enough for most purposes. Be sure to get waterproof board. Although slightly more expensive, it will hold up better in an automobile. Some upholsterers prefer $1/8$ inch thick composition board such as Masonite, or wood wall paneling, both of which offer greater stiffness.

Pattern

Lay the panel board on the worktable and trace the outline of the old panel onto it along with locations

Panel board can be cut to shape with heavy upholstery shears. A saber saw can be used for Masonite.

A punch starts the window crank hole, which can then be cut with shears or a utility knife. The initial hole can be started by drilling if no punch is available.

of all hardware and attachment holes. Cut out the new panel board, and cut or drill the holes where marked.

If you have no old panel from which to make a pattern, or the new panel has different dimensions, make a pattern out of a piece of heavy, clear plastic. Secure it over the door with masking tape, then trace the outline 1/8 inch inside the door edge. Mark all holes for hardware and attachment clips. Cut out the pattern, place it on the panel board and trace around it. After cutting the board, sand the edges so they won't wear through the covering.

Hardware and padding

Hidden spring clips are the most satisfactory for securing the panel to the door. The most popular type has a U-shaped portion that grips the panel board and a diamond or Christmas tree–shaped spring portion that fits into a hole in the door skin. Select one with the correct grip range to hold the panel snugly and still allow for the amount of padding between the panel and the door. Notice that these clips have a 1/2 inch offset, so the holes in the panel must be offset the same amount from the holes in the door. Try the bare panel for fit on the door, and make any adjustments before installing upholstery.

In Chapter 4 I covered the steps for attaching upholstery directly to a door or side panel, putting the design in and building up the padding at the same time. If that's your approach, go back to that section for finishing the panel. Here, I'll cover the installation

Punch out trim strip holes as well.

of a single piece of covering or one already cut and assembled into one piece.

Unless the covering already has a padded backing, apply padding directly to the panel board. Cut a sheet of foam 1/4 inch to 1/2 inch thick to the size and shape of the panel board. A soft foam padding can be folded over the edge of the board along with the cover, so it should be cut to overlap the board about an inch on all sides. If thicker or firmer material is used, however, cut it only 1/8 inch beyond the edge of the panel board to overlap just enough to form a protective cushion around the edge of the board for the fabric.

When correctly trimmed and positioned, cement the foam to the board with trim adhesive. Holding the padding in place, fold half of it back, spray adhesive on the other half and on the board, then carefully fold the foam into place and press down. Repeat with the other half of the foam. Cut out all trim holes with scissors. Then draw the design of your covering onto the foam, either from paper patterns or the finished covering. This will help you line up the design exactly when the covering goes on.

Covering

A plain piece of fabric or one already made up with a design must first be laid out and trimmed to size. A plain covering can be laid on the worktable face down and the panel board placed on top of it, lining up two square sides one to two inches from the edge of the material and drawing around the other sides, leaving a similar width for folding over and attaching.

If the fabric has a woven-in pattern or design, or pressed or sewn pleats, diamonds or squares, lay it face up on top of the panel board and move it around until the best position is determined. The design or pattern should begin at the top and at the most visible edge and be square with the panel.

Once positioned for best appearance, the material is folded back one half over the other, adhesive is applied to both surfaces, and the cover is carefully pressed down. Then the other half is folded back and the same procedure followed to glue it. The cover may be trimmed to one or two inches beyond the edge of the panel board at this point.

With the panel turned over so the covering is face down, pull the fabric over the top edge of the board and tack it into place with staples short enough that they won't penetrate entirely through the board. Begin at the center and work out in both directions, placing staples at one-inch intervals.

Align the front portion of the cover and glue in place first. Then fold back the cover material and apply adhesive to the rearward portion. Allow the adhesive applied to both surfaces to become tacky, then pull the cover over and press into place.

For a side panel to be covered with material that has already been sewn with rolls and pleats, measure from the forward end and draw a line which will align with the first pleat of the cover.

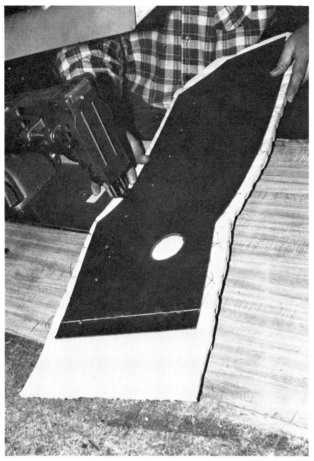

Sew the padded cover and board together around the perimeter. If a machine is not used, the edges of the cover can be pulled over and stapled.

Set the trim into place and secure the attachment prongs in back.

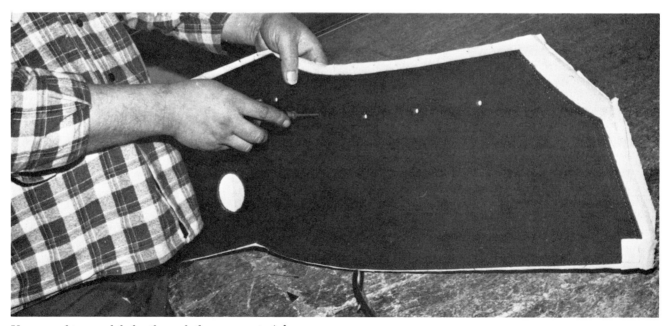

Use an awl to punch holes through the cover material.

Trim the cover to the edge of the panel board. If not sewn to the panel board as this one is, trim the foam to just beyond the edge of the board. Then pull the cover material over the edge and secure it by gluing, stapling or both.

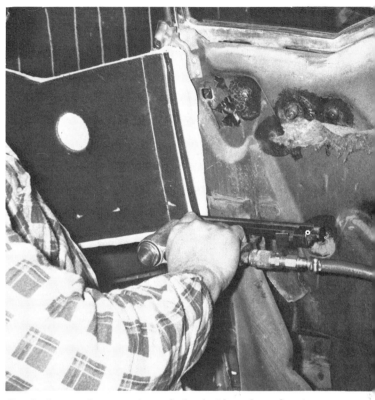

Staple the attachment strip on the back side to the tack strip just behind the door opening. When the panel is swung around into place, the staples are hidden and the front edge of the panel is neat and clean.

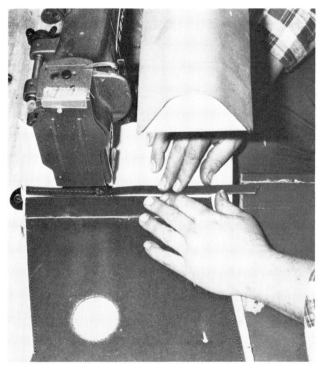

Since this panel attaches to a tack strip, sew a vinyl strip to the cover material at the front edge before surplus material is trimmed off. This strip forms a sort of hinge by which the panel attaches to the tack strip.

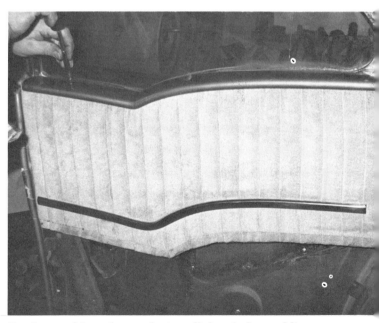

Set the panel into place and reinstall the window molding. The old, cracked windlace still needs to be replaced. The armrest and lower portion of this 1956 Chevy hardtop rear quarter panel were being refinished separately in a different material.

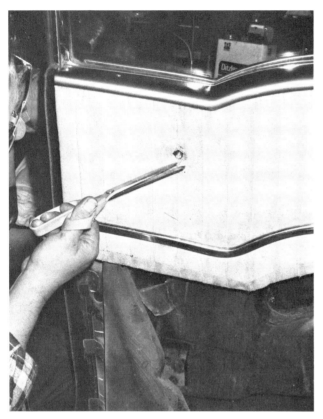

Locate the window crank hole and trim material out of it.

To make a new vinyl cover with top-stitched pleats to re-cover a door panel with a depression molded in, first apply glue, then use a board and lead weights to press the cover firmly into the depression while the glue dries.

With the window crank replaced, the job is complete. Note that windlacing, finished in contrasting velour, has now been installed as well.

114

Brush glue onto the metal lip on the bottom of the door panel and onto the vinyl cover material.

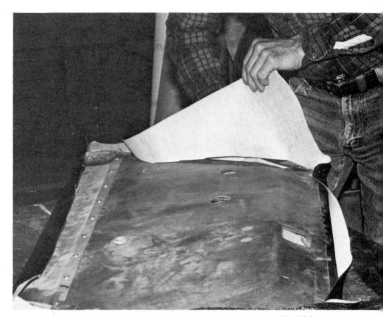

Stretch the material over the panel edges. If the panel will be subjected to stress and the edges not secured by trim, gluing these edges would be a good idea.

Turn the material over to check and see that any seams, designs or character lines in the covering are lined up correctly. Then go back and staple the bottom edge as you did the top, followed by the sides. Be sure to stretch the cover snug as you go.

Go back and staple solidly around the perimeter 1/4 inch to 1/2 inch from the edge of the board at intervals of 1/2 inch to one inch.

If the cover material is heavy, trim some of it away in the corners or make pie-shaped cuts so it will fold over neatly with only one or two layers to staple through. To finish off, the excess material is trimmed about 1/4 inch from the staple line.

Press the material onto the panel lip when the glue becomes tacky. Hold the material in place until it is securely set.

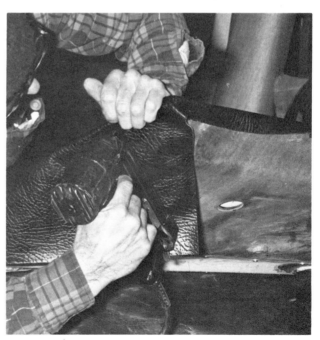

Staple the material in place, tacking one area at a time. Pull the material taut and hold with a staple, alternating sides and checking frequently to see that the front face is smooth.

Finish by stapling around the entire border at intervals of 1/2 inch to one inch.

Trim the excess material 1/4 inch from the staple line.

Installation

Locate holes for the handles, armrest attachment screws and any other door trim, and make small cross-cuts for them. Attach trim and any hardware such as window and mirror controls and courtesy lights to the door panel. Install the spring clips on the back. To

Corners may require that several tucks be made and stapled. If the material is quite heavy, make small cuts to allow the material to overlap as it is pulled tight to make a smooth corner.

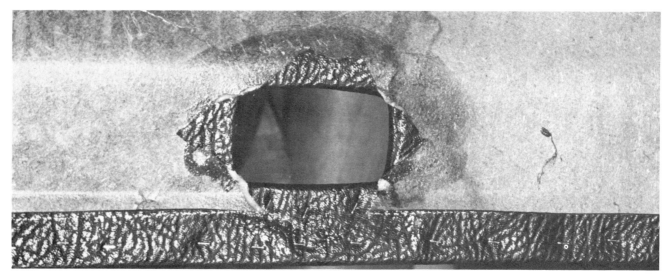

Cut cover material in a cross pattern for the door grip hole or any other openings required in the panel. Fold back the flaps through the opening, and fix with glue.

reinstall the panel, reverse the removal procedure. Feel behind the panel to guide each spring clip into the correct hole, then seat it in place by a firm push or a sharp blow with the heel of the hand.

Windlacing

Many trim suppliers offer windlace material by the roll finished in a variety of colors and fabrics. If there is not an exact match for your upholstery, a selection to closely coordinate or contrast may be found. However, making your own matching windlacing isn't difficult.

Get a roll of windlace core rubber from an upholstery supplier (1/2 inch diameter vacuum hose from an auto supply store will work). Cut strips of fabric four inches wide to wrap around the core with a double-

The finished panel is ready to install.

If working with a new fiberglass or old wood-framed body, you'll have to work out a means of attaching the upholstered panels. One way is to screw flat washers to the wood frame to receive spring clips.

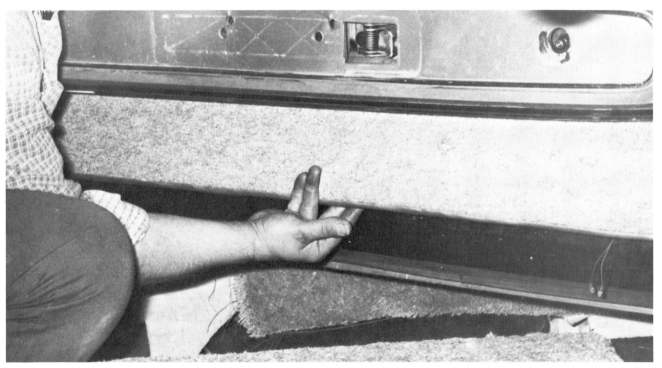

You'll be working "blind" when installing an upholstered panel to the door or body. Locate the clips one at a time, align them with the holes and bump the panel with the heel of your hand to set them in place.

118

thickness flap. To make strips long enough to go all the way around a door opening, sew two or more strips of fabric together. Cut the ends at a forty-five-degree angle, place them face to face with the ends even and sew across 1/4 inch from the edge. The resulting straight seam will be scarcely visible on the finished job.

Apply trim adhesive to the back side of the strip, lay the core in the center and wrap the fabric around it, lining up the edges and pressing them together. If an industrial sewing machine is available, the fabric may be sewn around the core rather than glued. Finish off one end by folding the material over and gluing. Ends of the windlacing are usually hidden behind seats or door sills, so you may want to wait until it's installed to finish trimming the ends. Trim the flap to leave about 3/4 inch for attachment.

Installation

When installing windlacing, keep in mind its purpose of sealing the interior against outside air, dust and moisture, and be sure to place it where it will be

Windlace seals the front opening and should fit snugly against the door upholstery when the door is closed.

On this 1951 Ford the windlace attaches with both tacks and metal grips.

most effective. Notice the method of attachment when removing the old lacing; it may be a combination of tacks, staples, clips, screws or molding.

Hold the strip of windlace in place and mark positions where sharp bends will be made to go around corners. Allow a little extra length to tuck under door sills or carpeting, then cut the windlace to the necessary length. Where the lacing bends around corners, make crosscuts or pie-shaped cuts at 1/2 inch to one-inch intervals to prevent bunching.

Install the windlace by stapling or tacking or other original attachment method, starting at one end and working around the opening. Trim excess material from the ends.

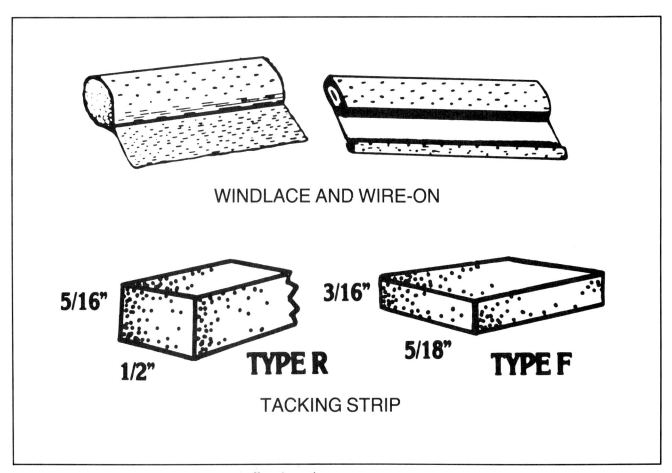

Kanter Auto Products offers replacement windlace in various colors as well as tacking strips for attachment.

Chapter Seven

Carpeting

Even in the days when the average new car came with rubber mats, builders of custom cars and street rods considered a nice layer of carpet on the floor a necessary part of the custom treatment. It not only gives the car a finished look and comfort underfoot, but it also aids in muffling noise and insulating the interior against heat and cold. Carpet material can also be decorative when added to the bottoms of door and side panels, kick panels, seat bolsters and even to cover package shelves.

Characteristics

As with upholstery fabric, carpeting has specific characteristics when made for automotive applications, since it must withstand exposure to extremes of heat and cold, certain wear patterns and moisture. Some household carpeting, though similar in composition and appearance, is unsuitable for a vehicle. To be safe, specify automotive carpeting, or deal with a firm that specializes in automotive trim materials.

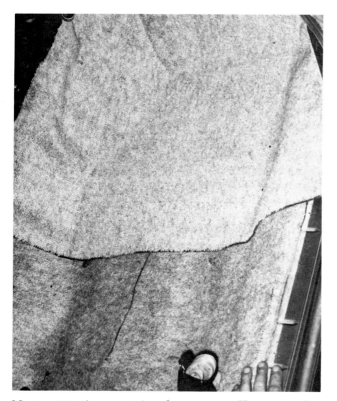

Most automotive carpet is nylon or rayon. Here new nylon loop pile is being installed over new insulation.

Loop pile, shown here, and cut pile are the most common choices. The pile can vary from short to long in either form.

LOOP PILE

CUT PILE

The difference between loop pile and cut pile is as their names state. Loop pile has continuous, looped strands; cut pile has the strands cut individually.

Most auto carpeting is nylon, which has a very nice appearance and wears well. Color selection is great, and it is reasonably priced. Some carpeting is woven of rayon alone or rayon blended with nylon.

Because of its quality and exclusivity, wool carpeting is preferred by some custom car builders. Once the principal carpeting fiber, today it is found only in the most expensive foreign cars. Wool has excellent durability, a rich texture and a subdued, not shiny finish. It is also costly.

Pile

The other characteristic of carpet, in addition to fiber, that needs to be understood is pile. The pile is the nap of the carpet, the exposed surface, and it determines how the carpet looks and feels.

The pile consists of threads or yarn woven in loops and bonded to a woven backing. If it is left this way, the carpet is known as loop pile. The pile may be low or nearly flat, or the loops may be longer for a deeper pile. In some instances the loops are formed into rows to

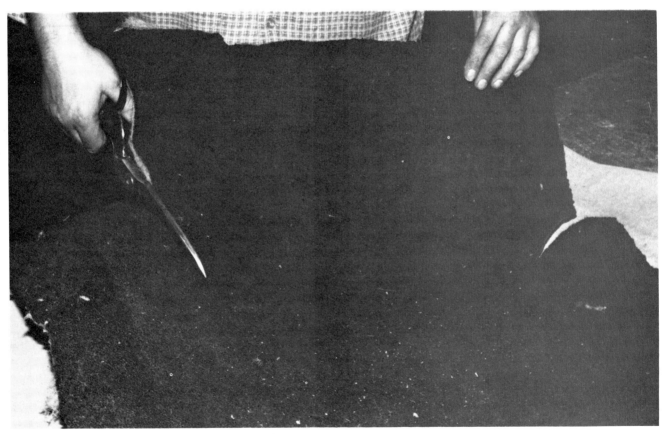

To use an old molded carpet as a pattern, cut each corner where it dips down. This will allow the old carpet to lie flat.

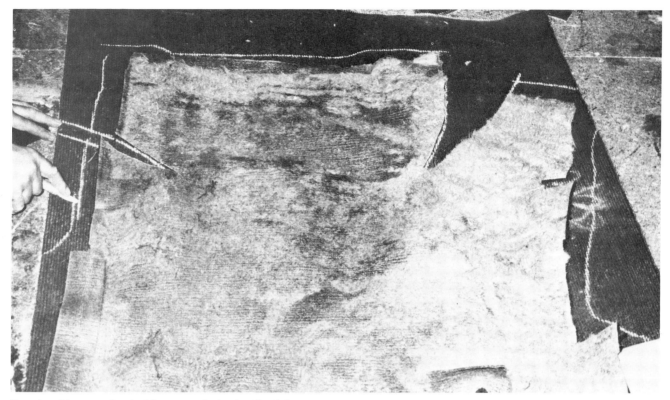

Lay the old carpet, back side up, on the back side of the new carpet and trace around it, leaving one to two inches extra around the borders.

create a ribbed pattern, but most of the time they are random so the surface is uniform. Carpet woven with loops of varying lengths to create a sculptured pattern usually is more appropriate for a household than for an automotive application.

To create cut pile carpeting, the ends of the loops are shaved off, leaving the fibers sticking up like brush bristles. Again, the pile may be short or deep, depending on the depth of the loops to begin with. A deeper pile lends a softer, plusher feel to the interior, but is prone to mat down. It is also more difficult to keep clean because bits of sand and dirt go so far down into the pile that a vacuum cleaner has trouble reaching them.

With both loop pile and cut pile carpet, the tighter the weave, the firmer and more durable it will be. As with upholstery material, the choice will depend somewhat upon the style of the interior. The deeper cut pile carpeting has come into favor in recent years and is more suited to a modern interior, while short cut pile and loop pile are more in keeping with earlier styles.

Fitting

When preparing carpet, begin with a clear floor with seats and all hardware removed. Be sure the

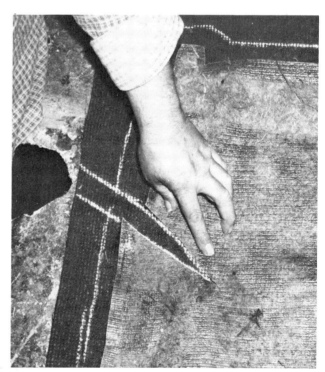

Mark the spots where the old carpet was cut so they can be cut out of the new carpet in the exact location.

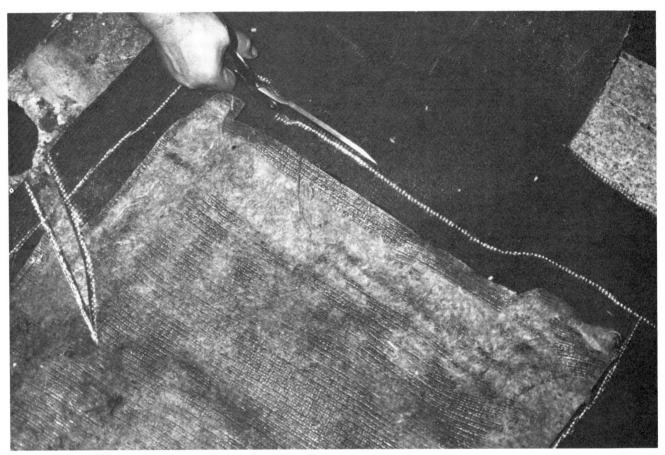

Cut out the new carpet on the marked lines, including the V-shaped cuts for the corners.

Sew the V-shaped corner cuts together by folding the sides of the cut together, face to face, and stitching about 1/4 inch from the edge. This will pull the carpet together at the correct points to make it fit the floor shape.

floor is thoroughly cleaned and, if necessary, refinished with a rust-inhibiting paint. Making a pattern can be difficult. Using the old carpet or mat is best. Otherwise, an old sheet may be laid over the floor and marked for the outside boundaries and where cuts must be made for pedals, the transmission hump and seat brackets. Making separate pieces for front and back floors, meeting underneath the seat like most factory jobs do, will make the job easier.

Transfer the pattern to the carpet material and cut it out with a sharp utility knife. Leave plenty of extra material on all sides; you can trim it after all other fitting is done. You may wish to fit the carpet into the car to mark directly on it where the cuts must be made. The upper part of the transmission tunnel is the most difficult. Determine the approach that will require the slightest amount of cutting and fitting. Chances are, the best way will be to make the main body of carpeting cover the floor, sloping floorboards and straight parts of the driveshaft tunnel, then cut a separate piece to fit over the transmission hump where it slopes up and widens under the dashboard. Where cuts are necessary to go around pedals, make a single cut from the top edge of the carpet to the pedal location, then enlarge the hole around the pedal and the carpet will lie flat, the nap hiding the cut.

Binding

Most carpeting doesn't require binding because the edges are hidden under door sill plates and uphol-

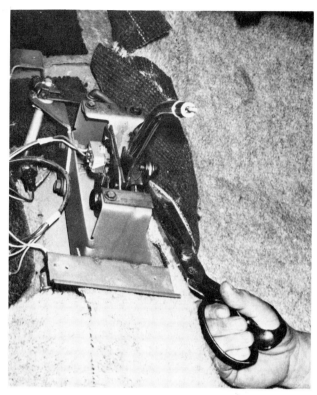

Put the carpet into the car for a trial fit. When it is lying in the desired position, trim it as necessary to fit around gearshift mechanisms and pedals. Holes must also be made for seat and seatbelt attachments.

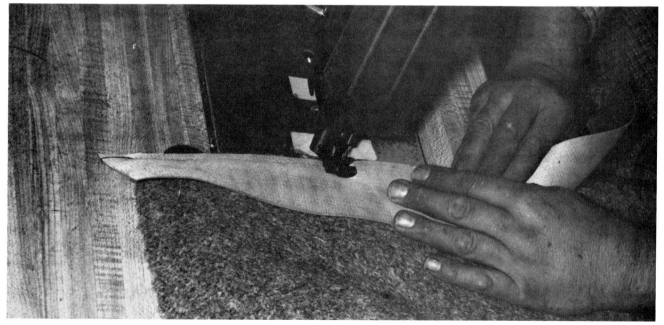

Determine what edges will be exposed; usually it will be an edge where the front section overlaps the back. There may also be places where the carpet has to be cut to fit over the transmission hump, and on some installations the side and front edges may be exposed rather than tucked under trim and sill moldings. Sew a length of vinyl to the edge as a binding.

After first being placed face to face with the carpet and sewn ½ inch from the edge, the vinyl binding is pulled around the edge and sewn just inside the first seam to secure the binding on the back side. The carpet pile will hide the seam.

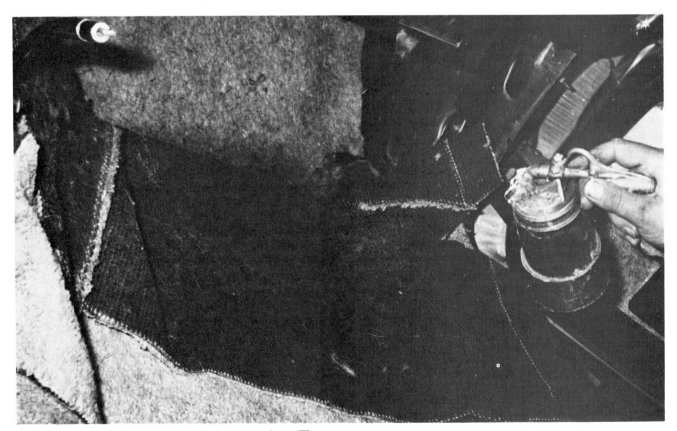

Put the carpet in place to see that it fits everywhere. Then fold the front half back and coat both the floor and back of the carpet with adhesive.

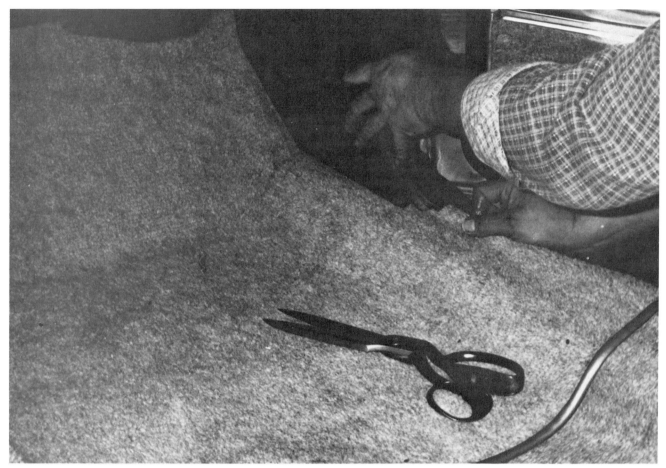

Press the front half in place. Repeat the gluing procedure on the back half and press it down.

stered panels. If binding is required, however, it is done with a strip of upholstery material, usually vinyl in a matching or contrasting color, cut two to three inches wide.

Place it face down on the carpet with the edges aligned and sew together about 1/2 inch from the edge. Then fold the binding material over, right side out, pull it snugly around the edge of the carpet and sew a second time as close as possible to the fold in the binding. Sewn with a matching thread color, the seam will pull down into the carpet and be nearly invisible. If the backing is not too tough, however, you can attach the binding to the bottom of the carpet with a blind stitch by hand-sewing it with a curved needle.

Installation

A sheet of carpet padding, usually an inch thick, should be cut to the size and shape of the carpet, leaving an inch of carpet exposed where it has to tuck under the door sills. Bond the padding to the back of the carpet with adhesive. An alternative approach is to cement the padding to the floor first and put the carpet

in place over it. When it is properly fitted, fold back half of it at a time, spray adhesive onto both the carpet and the padding and smooth the carpet into place. Repeat with the other half of the carpet.

Some final trimming may be necessary as the carpet is tucked into place.

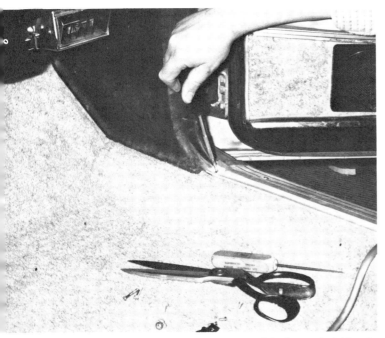

Replacing the door sill molding and kick panels hides the carpet edge. Use an awl to locate screw holes.

Secure rubber or vinyl heel pads or other similar inserts in place by shaving away the pile where the pads fit, and cementing them to the backing.

The carpet edges are tucked under trim panels where required and secured on the sides by replacing the door sill plates and other hardware.

Ready-to-install carpet

The growing number of material suppliers serving the auto customizing and restoration fields has given a real boost to the availability of ready-to-install carpet. Several of the sources listed in the Appendix offer precut, ready-to-install carpet for a large number of car and truck models, the more popular ones from as early as 1928. Some offer strictly original, replacement-type carpet, while others have custom carpet kits in a choice of materials and styles. Either may be satisfactory in a custom application as long as the floor has not been altered.

Especially convenient and cost efficient for later model cars with wells in the floor is carpet molded to the exact shape for the particular model. Cutting and shaping carpet for these irregular floor shapes can be difficult.

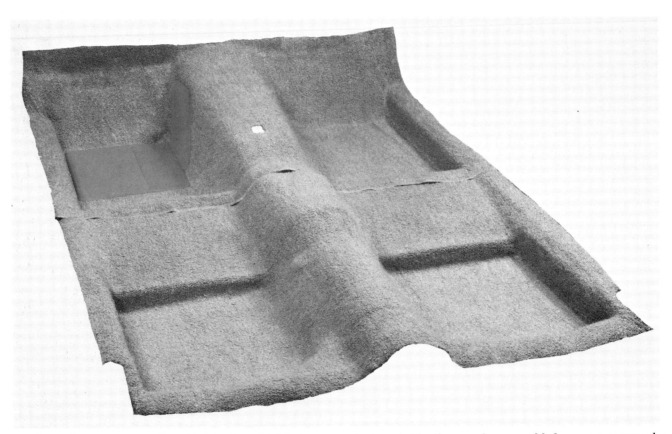

Ready-made carpet cut and molded to the vehicle's floor shape is available for many models from firms like Auto Custom Carpet. If the floor is quite irregular with sunken foot wells like the one shown, molded carpet can save the considerable work required to cut and fit flat carpeting.

Chapter Eight

Choosing seats

As with the couch or your favorite recliner in the living room, the seats are the most important part of your car's interior. They have to look good, and since you'll be spending a lot of time in them, they'd better be comfortable, too.

Various seating arrangements were discussed in Chapter 1, so if you've been planning your interior layout, you already know whether your seating will be bucket or bench, traditional or modern. You also have some other choices to make.

Keep the original seats

Take a look, first, at the present seats in your car. Are they in the seating configuration you want? Are they the right style and reasonably comfortable? What condition are they in?

If the arrangement and style are suitable, stock seats are a pretty good starting point. Built up or re-padded to improve comfort, they can be restored to new condition or better. Beginning with the original seats will save you the bother of searching out and installing replacements, which themselves may have to be reupholstered.

Find different seats

Perhaps you have your mind set on a particular seat. Many improvements have been made in appearance, comfort and safety over the years. If units from another model are in your interior design, installing them in your car doesn't have to be a difficult operation.

Take measurements

Begin with measurements of your car. The most important is the distance between the mounting tracks. Installation will be easier if replacements have the same or nearly the same measurement. Then the new seat or at least one of the two tracks on bucket seats can bolt into the same place. Some cars have re-

inforced floor pans where the seat tracks bolt on, so it's important to try to bolt the new seats into the same area.

Measure the distance from door to door so you know the maximum space available for the new seat. Also measure the maximum height of the drive-shaft tunnel from the floor, since the seat must clear it in the middle. Later model seats are built low and mount

Original seats are a good base to start from for building a custom interior if they can be rebuilt and re-covered to your satisfaction. The one in this 1946 Mercury was refinished in diamond-tufted Naugahyde.

This very serviceable set of leather seats was rescued from a Chrysler headed for the crusher.

More popular as custom replacements than bench seats, bucket seats command higher prices at the salvage yard.

close to the floor, so when they are put into an earlier model, the mounting has to be built up.

There are several ways this can be done. A solid piece of wood cut to provide the necessary amount of lift can be placed between the seat mount and the floor with longer mounting bolts passing through it and attaching to the floor, or the wood riser bolted to the floor and the seat bolted to it. More rigid than wood, but applied in the same way, would be a length of steel tubing or U-channel of the correct dimensions. It may also be possible to modify or extend the seat mounting brackets to provide the additional height required.

Aftermarket seats

Several companies sell special seats for street rods, customs and street machines. Most of these are bucket models designed for performance and comfort with high backs, headrests, body-supporting bolsters and adjustability for increased support when and where it's needed. Back seats designed for certain popular sedans but adaptable to others are also available. Some of the suppliers are listed in the Appendix.

If you plan to install a modern aftermarket seat, how it's finished will determine how the rest of the interior is trimmed. Usually, a choice of finish is offered

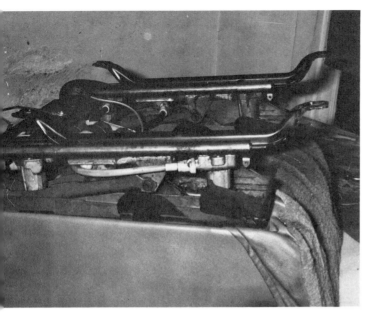

A power-controlled seat mechanism like this will readily adapt to many situations. The U-shaped mounting brackets are held to the floor by four bolts.

The rear mount had to be altered and extended to fit this late-1960s bucket seat to a 1955 Chevy floor pan. The channel iron extension was welded to the original bracket.

Bob Sipes custom-built these Corvette seats for his custom 1949 Ford. The framework was rebuilt so the seat backs fold at a higher point.

A custom seat in a fiberglass street roadster was constructed of blocks of foam and permanently fixed to the floor and back panel of the passenger compartment.

from a wide variety of styles, colors and fabrics, including cloth, vinyl and leather. The same supplier may furnish matching material for trimming the rest of the interior, or you can find one that closely matches or harmonizes.

Custom seats

Sometimes a builder will create a custom car which requires custom-designed seating to fit its special interior layout, or because ready-made seating simply doesn't go along with the design. The popular T-bucket roadster is an example. Although seats are available to fit them, these fiberglass bodies often are modified to the point of requiring a special seat.

The key to designing a custom seat is to make it comfortable for the driver and passengers and integrated into the interior design of the car. Most of these are permanently mounted and not adjustable, so it's very important to set them at the correct height and distance from the controls so the driving position will be comfortable on long trips. Stack slabs of wood to sit on and keep adding until the seating height is where you want it in relation to the steering wheel and other controls, windshield and top. Then measure the height from the floor to arrive at the height of your finished seat.

At the same time, measure from the floor to a point just behind the knee on the back of the leg to get the height the front of the cushion must be to give you leg support. Measure from the back cockpit wall (in the case of a roadster) to your back at the top of the seatback, and also to your buttocks when you are in a comfortable posture, to determine the position and

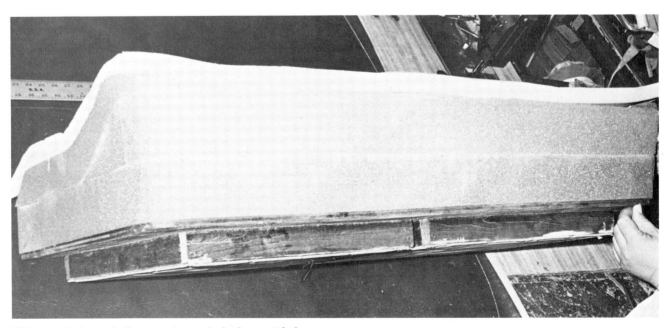

This seat is being built on a plywood platform with foam rubber built up in layers to the desired height.

Boxes dropped two inches below the platform and finished with webbing will provide extra cushioning for the bottom of this seat. The platform was cut out and additional foam cut to fit inside the boxes.

Seat risers in this street rod are constructed of one-inch-thick wood. In this view of the rear seat area, supports on each side and in the middle are shaped to fit, then bonded to the fiberglass floor. The front of the seat riser, with stereo speakers mounted behind cut out holes, attaches to the supports with angle brackets.

Using an electric carving knife is an easy way to cut and shape blocks of foam.

angle for the backrest. You may wish to place a board vertically to lean against and block it into the proper position and angle to take measurements.

Another measurement should be from the outside edge of the cockpit to the center of the steering wheel to set the center of the driver's seat. The passenger seat will be a corresponding distance from the right side.

Following these measurements, make a pattern on a piece of heavy paper for the seat framework. The pattern is then traced onto a sheet of 1/2 inch plywood, and the individual components (back, seat and sides) are cut out with a saber saw. Sand the edges smooth.

The riser on which the seat frame rests is most easily cut out of one-inch pine and put together like a box. You may want to make the front panel of the riser removable and attach it to the sides with screws or L-shaped brackets so you can mount stereo speakers behind it. In a fiberglass car, the seat riser may be bonded to the floor, and possibly the sides of the body with epoxy and fiberglass mat or with an adhesive (like Liquid Nail). It will probably be bolted to the floor in a steel car.

When cut to near the desired shape, test the seat fit.

Another way of building a custom seat is to modify a steel seat framework and springs to fit your compartment. Measure the seat framework to determine how much to cut it down. With a hacksaw or cutting disc, remove the unneeded length from the middle of the framework, line up the remaining sections and weld them together. Cover the framework with burlap and foam, building up certain portions with extra foam if desired, and finish it with your cover material.

Padding

Building up the plywood seat frame can be done quite satisfactorily with foam rubber. The secret of building a comfortable seat is to make the cushion, in particular, as high as space will allow. That doesn't mean it must be soft; the density of the padding will determine how soft or firm it is, but the more padding you use, the less likely you are to "bottom out" on the seat frame when you hit a bump, or to become fatigued on a long drive.

Minimum padding of medium-density foam on an unsuspended (no-springs) seat should be three to four inches on the cushion and two to three inches on the back. You may wish to build it up more around the edges for additional leg and lateral support and to create more of a bucket effect.

Illustrated here is how the seats of a four-door phaeton street rod were fully contoured with foam before being covered with leather. Three-inch blocks of medium-hard foam were glued to the plywood base.

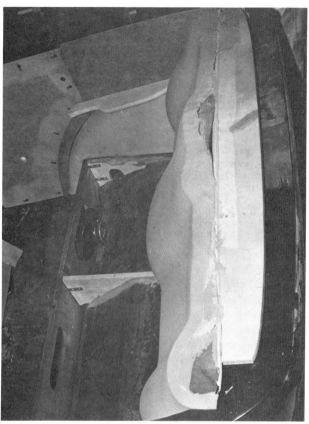

Form the sides and the center of the seat back into contours with extra foam padding. Glue the foam to the plywood seat back and build up in layers.

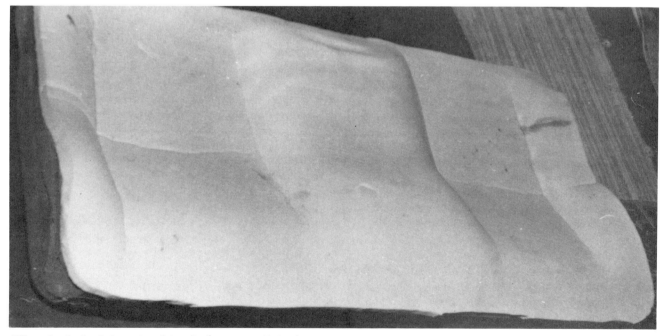

When the desired shape is achieved, glue a smooth top layer of soft one-inch foam on top as a base for the cover.

Additional foam was cut to rough shape and glued to the foam already in place, building up the sides, center, lumbar support and leg support sections of the seats. An electric carving knife was used for trimming and sculpting the foam. This job was done freehand by an experienced upholsterer; you'd be wise to follow a pattern, or shape one side of the seat, then make templates of several sections to help shape the other side to match.

When the desired shape was accomplished, a layer of one-inch medium-light foam was glued over the entire surface to provide a smooth, soft basis for the covering.

For this installation, another step was taken in the interest of driver and passenger comfort. Holes were cut out of the plywood base in the two seating positions and boxes constructed to drop those sections two inches below the level of the cushion base. Webbing such as that for repairing lawn chairs was fastened across the openings, and the boxes filled with foam padding cut to fit. An extra depth of padding on a nonrigid base is thus provided in the most critical parts of the seat.

The front seat of this 1934 Ford phaeton street rod is contoured for the owners' comfort.

Chapter Nine

Covering seats

Seat cover construction is the most complicated project in interior customizing. Although a good home sewing machine might handle the sewing requirements, a commercial machine is almost a must. There are occasional instances, such as those described in Chapter 4, in which a seat covering can be constructed directly on a wooden frame. Yet seat covers are not beyond the capability of the home craftsman, so don't be frightened off by the prospect. Just plan your work and take your time.

The "fitting dummy"

At this point you have some kind of seat to work with. It's either a new one you've built or an old one that came with the car, from a salvage yard or swap meet. The seat will serve as a fitting dummy; you can do all the design layout, measuring and fitting directly on it. If it's an old seat, leave whatever covering it has in place. That will hold the shape to make your measuring and fitting as accurate as possible.

Measure and mark the center line of each seat part with chalk as a reference point. Measure out and mark your pattern or design elements; for example, the locations of a pleated or tufted panel, the border and seams where various panels join. As you construct the seat cover, follow this layout in taking measurements and sewing panels together, and check the fit frequently.

As your new cover nears completion, it'll be safe to remove the old seat covering. Pay close attention to how it attaches. It may be a combination of hog rings, staples or tacks, metal clips or strips of plastic channel. The latter two must be saved for reuse. There may also be wires running through listing strips to help se-

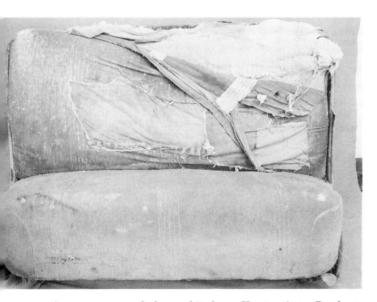

A presewn reupholstery kit from Kunler Auto Products turned the patched and frayed relic left into the like-new

seat right. Corduroy, broadcloth, mohair, velour and vinyl materials are offered in plain or pleated styles.

137

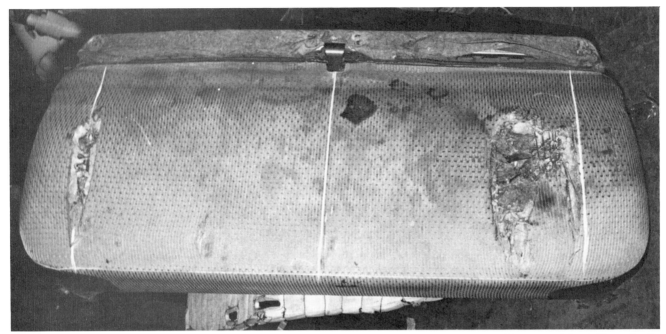

Unless it's completely dilapidated, your car's old seat can serve as a dummy for fitting the new cover. Mark your design layout directly on the old cover with chalk and take measurements from it.

cure the edges evenly. Save them, too. Make note of welt cord that may be sewn into the edge of the boxing to provide a better grip for the hog rings and "tails" used to secure the cover underneath.

Construction

For the sake of illustration, consider that the seat covering will consist of a central section in a roll-and-

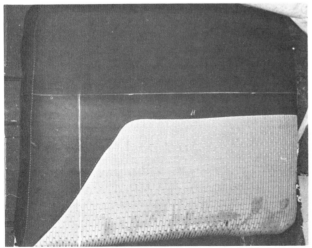

Indicate with chalk marks on the backrest the area to be covered by the rolled and pleated insert in the center and the top and outside panels to complete the cover.

pleat design, surrounded by a horseshoe of plain material. The same pattern will be repeated on the backrest. (The roll-and-pleat insert is constructed as outlined in Chapter 4.) The edge is sewn in the intended shape with a 1/2 inch flap for attaching it to the adjoining pieces.

The horseshoe might be cut in one piece, but in the interest of conserving fabric will probably be a front piece and two side pieces joined by seams at forty-five-degree angles at the front corners. The boxing that covers the front and sides of the seat cushion, again, may be one piece or a front and two side pieces sewn together.

Locate the center point of each piece by folding it in half, and mark it by making a small V-cut. In each instance when panels are sewn together, line up the center points and sew from there, first in one direction, then return to the center and sew in the opposite direction. This helps to even out any differences in the way the two materials stretch.

Welting is first sewn to the edge of the roll-and-pleat insert. It provides a guide for the machine when the horseshoe panel is then sewn on. Cutting each panel with the same 1/2 inch sewing allowance makes it easier to line up the edges and sew about 3/8 inch from the edge.

Welting is then sewn onto the outer edge of the horseshoe panel and, in turn, the boxing sewn to it. Some later styles eliminate this seam and continue the horseshoe panel over the edge of the cushion, attaching it to the frame below. Add any outer pieces the original cover may have had for attachment purposes or that would ease reattachment of the cover. These might include folding the bottom of the boxing around welt cord and sewing, or sewing a tail or a listing strip of a strong, inexpensive fabric on the back of the cover with a welt cord or wire to be hog-ringed to the frame.

The same procedure is followed to construct the cover for the backrest. In this case, a back must be added and all sewing done with the cover turned inside out.

Continuing the above example, the backrest cover, in order of attachment, would consist of a roll-and-pleat panel, a horseshoe panel, a top and side panel and a back panel. As with the cushion, some styles would combine the horseshoe and the top panel of the horseshoe and the side panels into one. Again, mark the center point and begin sewing from it to the outside in both directions. Welting would normally be used at each of the seams, as it was on the cushion.

When the backrest "envelope" is completed, turn it right side out. Again, there may be tails, listing strips, welt cord or wire to be added for attachment.

Padding

Foam is the logical choice for most seat padding because of its versatility, comfort, cost and durability. Padding with medium-firm foam will provide the necessary support. Add a bit more where seats may be sagging or in spots where you want more support. (Foam won't take the place of worn or broken springs, though, so install new ones as necessary.) A thin layer of softer foam provides a smooth cushion just under the cover to give the seat its final shape.

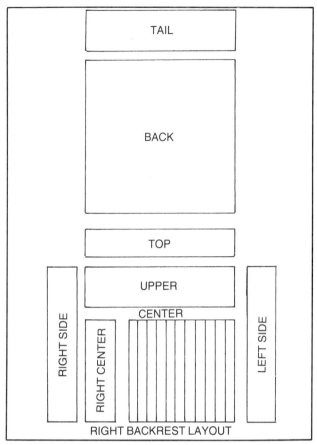

These pieces make up the right backrest of the front seat. The same components in reverse are required for the left backrest cover.

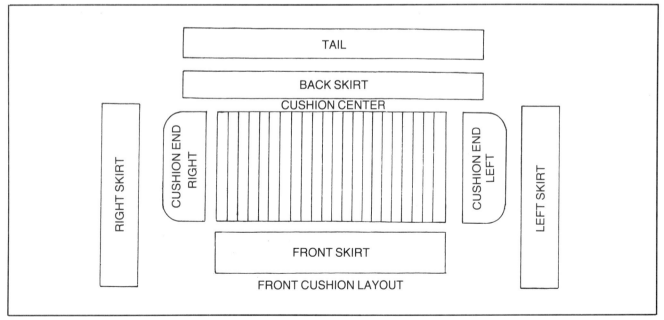

These are the separate components that must be made and joined together to make the cushion cover.

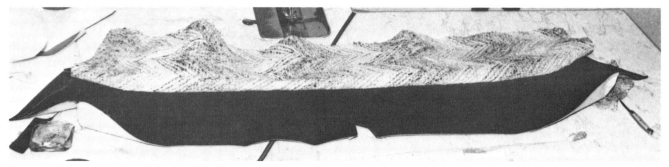

Notch the vinyl back skirt in the middle to fit around the backrest mounting bracket. The tail is a scrap of heavy fabric to secure the cover underneath. The tail won't be visible.

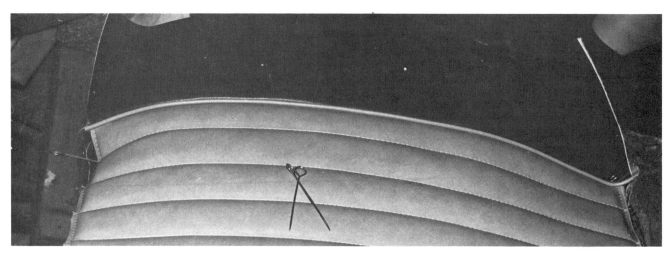

Sew the ends of the cushion cover to the roll-and-pleat panel with a welt between. Then fit the cover to the seat and hold it with upholsterer's pins.

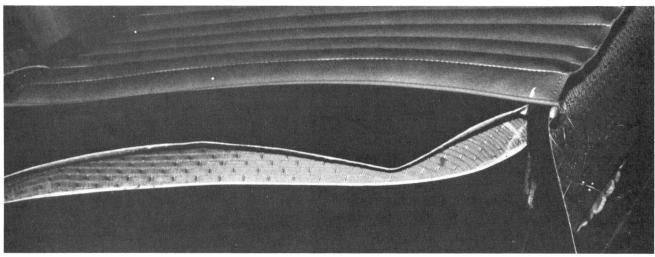

Cut material for the skirt to the approximate size, and pin in place. Trim both pieces to fit together evenly at the edge of the seat cushion. To make an identical skirt for the other end of the seat, either double the material when fitting it and cut both pieces at the same time, or use the first piece as a pattern to mark and cut the second.

140

If you're recovering a molded foam cushion from a late-model car, remember that foam that has become compressed with age can be rejuvenated with an application of steam. Also, worn-out foam or holes can be repaired by cutting out the old and cementing in a new piece of foam cut to shape. More specifics are in the discussion of foams in Chapter 3.

Installation

Done right, seat covers will fit tightly; you don't want wrinkles, either now or in a few months when they're broken in. You may wish to put a piece of muslin or paper cloth over the seatback to make it easier to pull the cover over the foam. Either before putting the cover in place or before attaching to the frame, check for any low spots or areas that need to be filled out a bit more, and stuff Dacron batting into them.

Lay the cover on the seat cushion, pull it into place on all sides and check for fit and position. Pull the cover down snugly in the middle at the front and attach it for position with one or two rings (or clips or whatever device is used). Then stretch it to the rear and secure it in the middle. Do the same on each side or end. Continue to stretch and secure a few inches at a time, alternating between front and rear, left and right, and working from the center toward the corners. You may need to take tucks or cut notches in the corners to make the cover attach smoothly.

The same system is followed for covering the backrest. Pull the cover into place and begin attachment in the middle, then work out to the sides a few

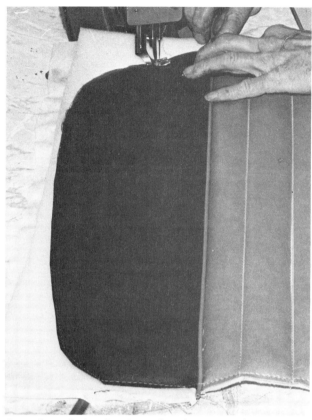

Once the end piece is trimmed to the correct shape, remove the cushion cover and sew the end piece to a piece of cloth-backed foam. Then, trim the foam to the edge of the cover and sew a welt to the border.

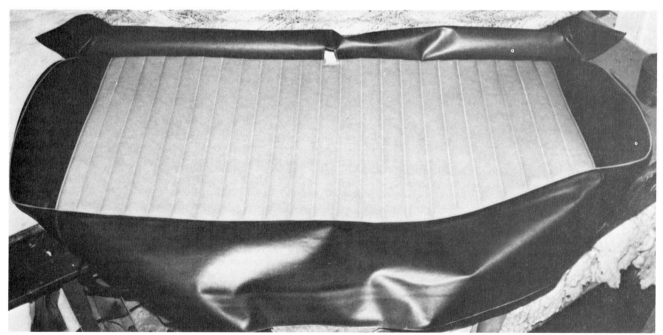

First sew the front skirt to the two side skirts, then sew the entire skirt panel to the cushion top panel with a welt be- *tween. Finally, add the back skirt, and the cushion cover is ready to install.*

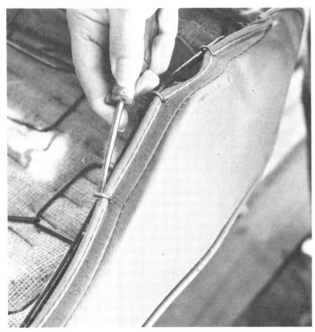

inches at a time, stretching the cover tight and attaching the rings or clips.

Your seats should look fresh and inviting and be ready for several more years of service.

Most older seat covers such as this one are attached with hog rings. Some later models have a plastic channel strip that fits over the seat framework.

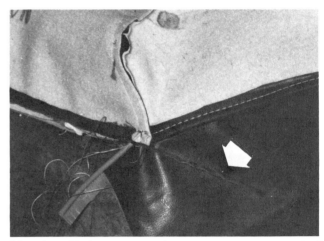

Many installations require a listing strip and wire attached to the back. This one on a 1955 Chevy front seat places the wire at the seam between the cushion top and the back skirt. The old wire can usually be reused.

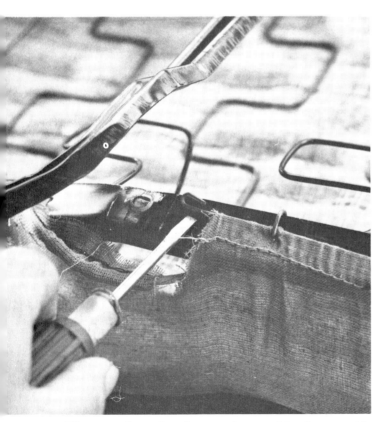

Wires run through a sleeve and secured by rings provide uniform tension on the back of the cover. Remove and reuse them on your new cover.

Secure the wire at the back of the cushion cover with hog rings to hold the cover snugly. Pull the back skirt over the back of the seat frame. Then pull the tail under and hog-ring it to the springs.

The cover is fitted all around. At this point Dacron filler could be stuffed under the cover if necessary to fill out any low spots.

Pull side and front skirts over the edge of the seat frame. Fold the edge back to form a double thickness and hog-ring to the frame. This seat frame has eyes to receive the hog rings.

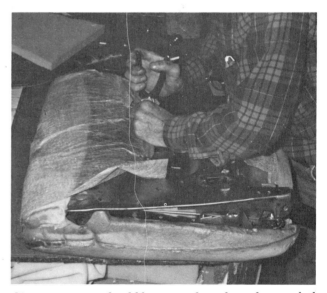

Since seat covers should be a snug fit, a sheet of paper cloth or muslin spread over the seat makes it easier to slide a cover on.

143

Even so, a good-fitting cover will take some pushing and pulling to put on. This new cover is being slipped onto the molded foam backrest of a late-model Oldsmobile.

Rods or wires run across the cushion and clamp to the zig-zag springs. The rods or wires spread the load and firm up a sagging seat.

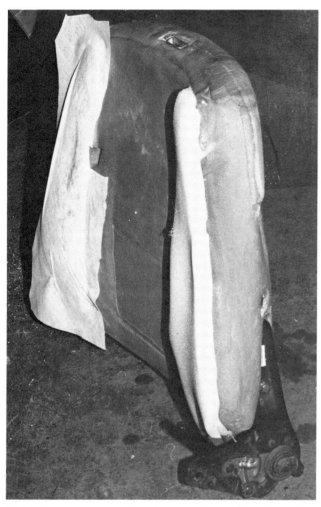

Molded-foam seats can be rejuvenated or built up by gluing new foam to damaged or depressed sections. Foam can be added in layers until the desired build-up is realized, then trimmed to shape with a hacksaw blade.

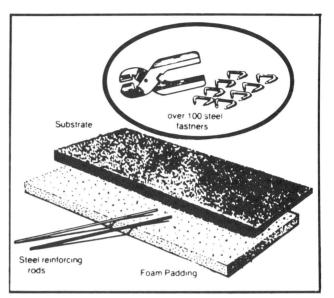

Seat rebuilding kits are available. Kanter Auto Products' kit contains steel rods to reinforce the springs, foam padding and a base for the cover, plus the fasteners for installation.

Careful planning and work will result in a set of comfortable and handsome custom seats. The covers on these original Mercury convertible seats have red velour roll-and-pleat panels surrounded by white vinyl borders in the classic horseshoe shape.

145

Chapter Ten

Kick panels and package shelf

The kick panels and the package shelf often go unnoticed. They usually blend in with the upholstery and carpeting, so you don't pay a whole lot of attention to them.

There's a possibility you won't have to pay attention to them in your custom upholstery job, either, provided they are in good shape and in a color to blend with the new interior. Many kick panels, in fact, are not upholstered, but are made of composite board or plastic with a texture to give them an upholstered look.

To make your interior complete and totally tied together, however, plan to finish off the kick panels and package shelf, too. They're not difficult jobs.

Kick panel construction

Remove the panels from the car and check their condition. Unless they're rotted or warped from moisture, broken or cracked, or have been butchered to install stereo speakers or other accessories, you can probably reuse them. Otherwise, trace around them onto a piece of upholsterer's panel board or Masonite and cut out the new boards. Masonite may not be flexible enough if the kick panel has much of a curve in it.

Decide before constructing or reworking kick panels what, if anything, will attach to them. A kick panel can be a handy, out-of-the-way spot for air-conditioner outlets, speakers or map pockets. Some already have air vents built in which you'll want to retain.

Work out and mark in chalk on the panel board the locations of any of these accessories, making sure

Making a heavy paper pattern of the space to be covered is the first step in making a kick panel if there is not an old one to work from. Cut the panel board to size and fit with the necessary attachment hardware. Then the panel can be covered and finished the same as door and quarter panels.

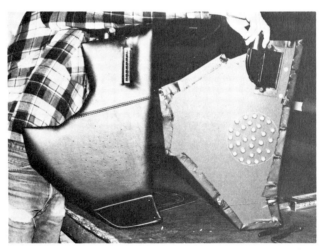

Custom-made kick panels can incorporate features such as air-conditioning outlets and stereo speakers. Air-conditioner outlets from a late-model car were fitted and cemented to these panels for a 1934 Ford street rod. Holes were punched into the panel board for the stereo speaker.

146

the necessary clearance is available behind them. Cut the holes with a utility knife or saber saw. The accessories may have provisions for screwing or bolting to the panel, or they may have to be attached with pop rivets or epoxy cement. A 1/2 inch punch is useful to make a pattern of holes in the panel for a speaker.

Upholstering

Installing upholstery on the kick panels will be similar to that of the door panels described earlier. The main consideration is whether to cover them in more than one kind of material. It may be that you'll want to follow through with the pattern from the doors, possibly with fabric or vinyl on the upper portions and carpet on the bottom, or with a roll-and-pleat or tufted motif. Plain fabric, vinyl or carpet matching the other interior materials work fine on kick panels.

Another consideration is whether or not to pad the panels. It's not necessary, but it will add some fullness that may be needed to blend with the rest of the interior.

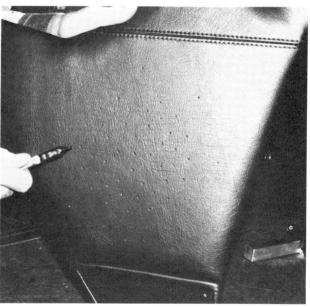

A geometric pattern was worked out on paper, then punched into the leather kick panel covers to emit sound from the stereo speakers.

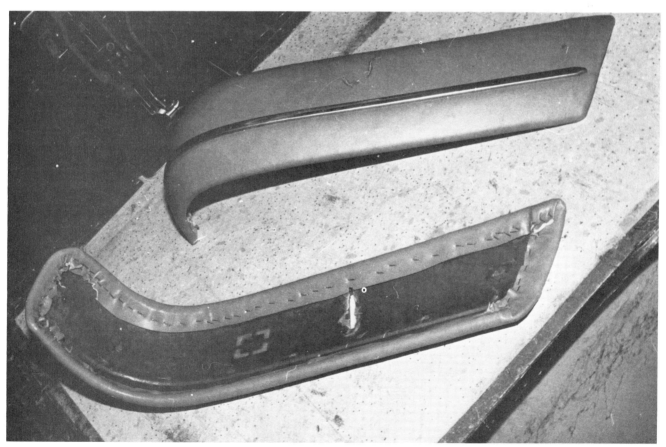

Some seat bolsters are finished with upholstery material. If they're not made to accommodate staples, the covers can be glued.

147

The rear package shelf comes out easily when the seat back and trim are removed. Trace around it onto the back of upholstery material matching the rest of the interior, allowing at least two inches in front and an inch on the other sides.

Glue the cover to the package shelf, pulling all edges except the front edge around and securing them on the back with glue and staples.

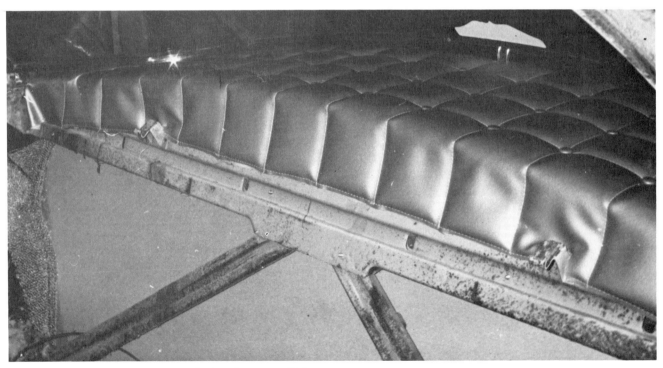

When the package shelf is reinstalled in the car, pull the cover down and glue it to the rear bulkhead.

Lay out whatever material you've chosen, including 1/4 inch or 1/2 inch foam if you've decided to pad the panels, and trace around the panel board onto the back side of the fabric. Pleated or tufted cover pieces may either be made up into a panel ahead of time or laid out and constructed directly onto the panel as described in the section on upholstering door panels.

Cut the material an inch or so outside the lines to leave material to pull over and attach. Mark and cut out any holes for accessories and hardware. Sound from the stereo speakers will carry through woven fabric, but it may be muffled by the foam padding, so this should be trimmed away in the speaker area. If the cover is vinyl or leather, work out a pattern that will enhance the design and punch small holes with a leather punch over the location of the speaker grille.

Position the foam onto the panel board, then while holding half of it in place, fold back the other half and spray a coat of adhesive onto both the panel board and the foam. When the glue becomes tacky, lay the foam in place and smooth it over that half of the board, then repeat the procedure on the other half.

Lay the cover material face down, and lay the board on it. Begin at one edge to pull the material over the board, and position it with staples or glue initially. Then stretch and attach the opposite side, followed by the remaining two sides, checking as you go to see that the material is even and unwrinkled on the finish side. After a final check, staple or cement solidly around the edge at 1/2 inch intervals.

Attach any accessories and hardware to the kick panel. Then install the panel back into place with whatever screws or clips secured it originally.

Building a package shelf

A fad of the 1950s and 1960s was the Naugahyde-upholstered package shelf. These were usually rolled and pleated, often with a candy-stripe pattern, except for the few that were button tufted to go along with the interior theme. They really stood out under the greenhouselike rear windows of those days.

Now not only are the rear windows less prominent, but the package shelf has nearly disappeared on some cars.

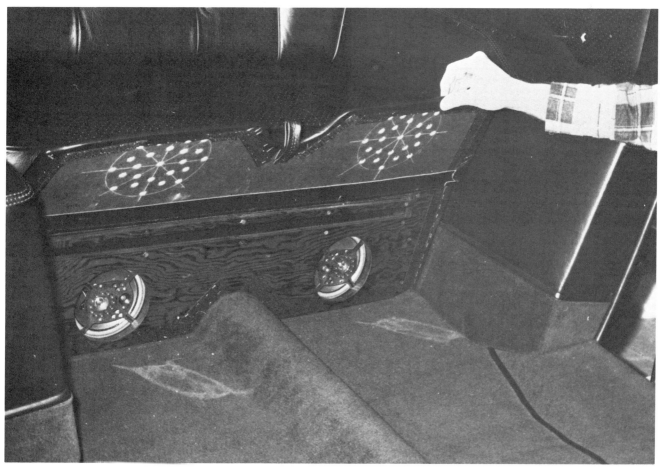

Speakers for this street rod are mounted behind the seat riser in the rear. A lift-up panel is punched with holes to let the sound escape, and the carpet finishing the outside of the panel is perforated with tiny holes like the kick panel above.

149

Go with the candy-stripe rolls and pleats or button tufting if you're following a period theme on a car from that era. Otherwise you may wish to choose something a little more subdued. A flat cloth or vinyl to match the seat cover and side panel material is always a good choice. Light, porous headliner material is also good. Even a cut, short-pile carpet works well on a package shelf. Anything you carry there will slide around, but not as much on woven fabric or carpet as on vinyl.

With the rear seatback removed, you can see how the package shelf is installed. Remove it carefully. Heat, cold and moisture often gang up on the composition material these pieces are made of, so it may be warped or rotted beyond further service. Still, you can trace a pattern from it onto a new piece of waterproof panel board, Masonite or thin plywood. Cut the new piece to shape with a saber saw or utility knife and check it for fit in the car.

The package shelf is a standard mounting spot for rear stereo speakers, so determine where they are to go. The whole appearance is neater if they are hidden under the shelf. The sound will carry through most woven materials well enough, but you'll have to perforate vinyl or leather as described for kick panels. The panel board must be marked and cut out over the speaker location, or perforated with a series of smaller holes as described earlier.

Upholstering

Installing upholstery covering on the package shelf is the same as for kick panels. A thin layer of $1/4$ inch foam may be glued to the board for extra padding and insulation if desired. It should wrap over the front edge of the shelf as a buffer between the board and the metal structure below, but the final cover will serve that function on the other three edges.

With the board as a pattern, trace the outline onto the back side of the cover material and cut out, leaving about four inches on the front edge and one to two inches on the other edges. Stretch the material over the back and sides and secure with adhesive. Leave the front edge loose at this point. When putting the shelf back in place, pull the front edge of cover material tight and secure it with adhesive to the steel structure to hold the shelf tight and rattle free.

Chapter Eleven

Trunk trimming

If you've applied the procedures discussed up to this point to your upholstery work, you won't have any trouble following through to customize the trunk compartment. The techniques are all the same as those for other elements of the interior, although they may be applied in slightly different ways.

First comes an assessment of what you may need or want to have in the way of trunk furnishings. Con-

You can go all-out to make the trunk compartment outstanding for shows. This 1957 Chevy has the name sewn into a vinyl panel at the back, decorative stitching and rolls and pleats in the side and deck lid liner panels, a decorated vinyl tire cover and carpet on the floor.

Cleaning supplies and tools can be hidden in the back corners of the trunk behind the removable panels. Upholstery material is usually glued to the wheelwell.

Tool pockets are built into this trunk side panel. The pockets can be made by attaching a piece of material to a backing, sewing in channels as if making pleats, but sewing solidly only along the bottom and leaving the top open.

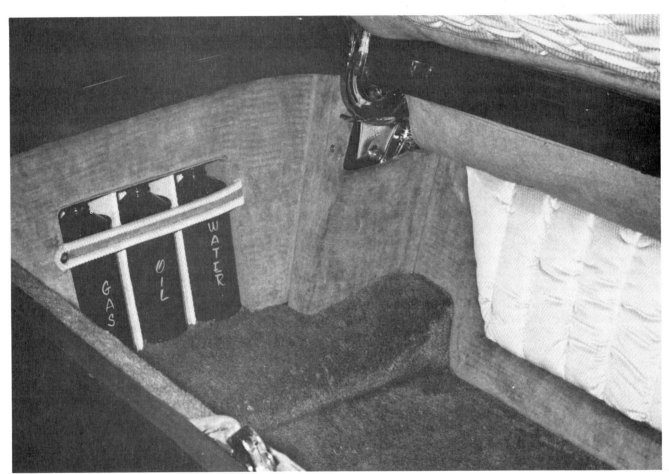

Compartments can be incorporated for spare fluid containers or emergency equipment. Here, a three-section box formed of panel board has been inserted into the trunk side

panel and fitted with a snap-secured strap to hold the containers in place.

sidering that it's principally a storage compartment, you may not wish to go beyond making it neat, clean and functional for carrying your suitcases and gear while traveling. Storage compartments for tools and emergency equipment can be provided and the spare tire covered. In this event, it may only be necessary to fit a nice piece of carpet on the floor and repaint the rest in the body color or with available crackle-finish trunk spray paint.

On the other hand, if you intend to open the compartment for inspection while showing the car, you may want to upholster the entire compartment. Usually this includes carpeting on the floor, fabric-covered panels on the sides and back wall, covers for the spare tire and battery or any other equipment stored in the compartment, and possibly a liner for the inside of the deck lid.

Carpeting

For the sake of continuity, it is advisable to get sufficient carpeting to cover the trunk at the same time you get it for the interior. It doesn't necessarily have to match, however. If you happen to get precut or molded carpet for the interior, the same supplier may have matching material by the yard for trunk and other trimming.

Consider unbacked carpet for the trunk. The woven pile without the backing is much more pliable

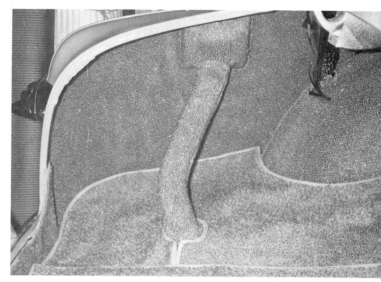

Unbacked carpet can be attached to the floor, tire wells and inner walls of the trunk with upholstery adhesive. In this Ford it is even wrapped around the gas filler tube.

and easy to work with in the tight corners and varied surfaces of the compartment. It can be cut, shaped, sewn and attached just like any other fabric. You can glue it right to the inside of the body panels, combine it

Unbacked carpet is nearly as pliable and easy to work with as upholsery fabric, so it's a good choice for finishing the trunk compartment. Cut to fit, individual panels can be bound with vinyl.

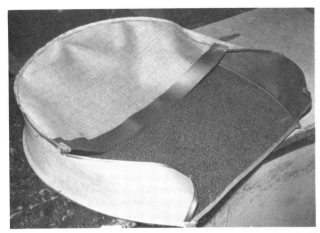

A tire cover consists of a carpet front, a rim and a half-envelope back of vinyl to slip over the spare tire. This one is shown inside out.

with other fabrics to make covers and stick insulation or padding to it to cover the floor.

Finding a close match to your interior carpet shouldn't be difficult. You may have to go to an upholstery shop or trim supply house to get unbacked carpet. Otherwise, auto supply houses often carry rolls of carpet material in a variety of colors, or a household carpet shop will have material to choose from. For the trunk it's best to stick with a short loop pile carpet for both appearance and ease of cleaning.

If intact, the original carpet or mat in the car's trunk will provide a pattern for the new carpeting.

Otherwise, make a pattern with heavy paper or plastic. Provided the floor is fairly regular without too many different levels and protrusions to work around, careful measuring will suffice. Transfer the measurements or pattern to the piece of carpet with chalk, doublecheck the measurements, then cut out the carpet with an inch or two to spare on all sides. It can be marked for more exact trimming when placed into the trunk for a trial fit.

The edges of the trunk carpet will probably need to be bound, since there is usually not any molding to hide them under. Cut a strip of your upholstery fabric or vinyl closely matching the carpet color and sew it to the carpet edge as discussed in Chapter 7.

Wait until the rest of the trunk upholstery elements have been constructed and installed before putting the carpet in permanently. Then fit it in place and fold back half at a time to apply adhesive to the cleaned trunk surface. Smooth the carpet into place and repeat with the other half. You may wish to consider installing snaps or strips of Velcro to make it easy to remove for cleaning, rather than permanently gluing the carpet in.

Side and back panels

There are two ways to approach the trimming of side and back panels of the trunk. One is to simply cover the stock panels or the exposed inside surfaces of the body panels themselves. The second is to construct panels to fill the spaces, upholster them and fit them to the compartment. A combination of the two approaches may work best. Although it is more work, the advantage of making new panels is that they can be designed to fit away from the compartment walls to make a neat padded box while allowing space behind to hide small items being carried in the trunk.

Join vinyl and carpet panels with welting to make up the tire cover. Add vinyl binding on the bottom of the carpet facing.

The center portion of the trunk floor carpet shown here is backed with insulation, which is glued to the carpet. The carpet can be glued to the floor or left loose.

Unbacked carpet with vinyl trim makes a neat finishing touch for the trunk. It will stand up to use and clean easily with a vacuum cleaner.

Applying fabric covering directly to the compartment walls requires that they be cleaned thoroughly to remove any grease and dirt, maybe even finished with a rust-inhibiting spray paint. Paper or scrap fabric is held in place and marked to make a pattern, which is transferred to the upholstery fabric and cut out with an allowance for final fitting and trimming. Vinyl, unbacked carpet or fabric with a tightly woven backing can be cemented in place directly, or the cover may be cemented to cloth-backed foam padding first for a smoother look. Fold over any edges that will be exposed and cement them or sew them for a finished appearance.

Upholstered trunk panels begin with a pattern for the area to be covered cut from heavy paper or light cardboard. Trace and cut out a piece of flexible panel board following the pattern. Using a less rigid material here should allow you to make panels that will flex enough to hold themselves in place. Try the bare panels in the trunk compartment and trim them to fit snugly before cutting them.

Place each panel on the upholstery fabric and draw around it, adding an attachment allowance of one or two inches on a side. Glue the cover and foam, if used, to the panel board and secure the edges with cement or staples on the back side.

A trunk lid liner is constructed like other upholstered pieces, but not backed by panel board so it can conform to the contours of the trunk lid. It is made of cover material sewn to cloth-backed foam. Various attachment means are available, including Velcro, snaps or sheet metal screws with snap-on covers upholstered in matching cover fabric, as used in the installation here.

155

Upholstery cover material can be glued to pliable panel board to make removable trunk side panels. Loops of cover

material can be attached to the back corners to provide a grip for removing the panels.

Upholstered panels hide the unsightly corners of the trunk. They cut down on usable space, but can also be used to hide tools and equipment.

An extra trick is to make a loop of the cover material one or two inches long and attach it as unobtrusively as possible to a corner of the panel. This gives you a grip to pull when removing the panel.

It may not be possible to wedge the panels into place where they'll be self-supporting. If necessary, braces or metal parts can serve as support. Drill small holes in the brace, punch corresponding holes in the panel and cover, and secure the panel with trim screws or button-head clips.

Panels for trunk and underhood areas can also be made up on a flexible backing of canvas or other string material for attachment with one of several kinds of fasteners. The male part of a snap is screwed into the body panel and the female portion secured to the cover. There are also screws to attach the cover semi-permanently, to which an upholstered head can be snapped on to lend a more finished look.

Glossary

Acrylic—a synthetic fiber with good wear characteristics found in many upholstery fabrics, especially as the surface fiber in a pile weave.

Batt, batting—a sheet of matted cotton used for padding and filling upholstered pieces.

Bench seat—a seat with a cushion extending the full width of the passenger compartment. A split bench is made in two individually adjustable sections without space between.

Biscuit tufting—a finish style with raised, padded tufts in a square or rectangular shape.

Blind stitch—a hand sewing technique started on the underside of the cover fabric and done so that the sewing thread is not visible on the finish side.

Burlap—coarse cloth woven from jute used as covering over springs to support layers of padding and stuffing.

Button tufting—a finish style in which covered buttons are inserted through the cover material and drawn down into the backing to create raised areas called tufts.

Channel, channeling—a finish design involving padding and shaping the cover material into a series of rounded, tubular sections vertically, horizontally or diagonally; more commonly known as rolls and pleats.

Coil spring—a seat spring of wire formed into a spiral.

Cotton—a fiber made from the cotton plant, woven alone or with other fibers into fabric. Also cotton batting, a mat made of cotton and other fibers for padding and filling upholstered units.

Cover—the outside or surface material on an upholstered piece.

Cushion—the surface of a seat on which one sits.

Dacron—trade name for DuPont's polyester fiber used for a variety of fabrics; also a material in mat form applied as padding or filler.

Density—the measure of the thickness of the cell walls of foam which indicates its durability.

Diamond tufting—a finish style with raised, padded tufts in a diamond shape.

Embossed—a fabric design raised from the surrounding surface.

Fabric—a cloth made by weaving, knitting or felting fibers.

Fiber—a fine, threadlike piece or slender filament, or matter composed of filaments.

Finish—the quality and appearance of the outer surface of an upholstery material.

Foam—a spongy, cellular, urethane-based material for shaping and padding upholstered pieces; short for foam rubber.

Headliner—the inside covering of the roof of a vehicle.

Hog ring—a fastener of steel wire in a C shape with sharp ends for attaching material to a seat frame or wire.

Hog ring pliers—a special tool with jaws designed to hold a hog ring and crimp it around a seat frame or wire.

Indentation load deflection (ILD)—a measure of the hardness of foam expressed in pounds.

Kick panel—the panel ahead of the front doors below the dashboard.

Listing strip—the fabric sheath by which a headliner is hung from steel bows.

Masonite—a wood fiber material pressed into sheets; one of several types of material for making panel board.

Mohair—originally a popular upholstery fabric made from Angora goat hair characterized by a thick, medium-length nap, generally replaced by synthetic materials with similar finishes which are referred to as mohair.

Nap—the short, fuzzy ends of fibers on the surface of cloth.

Nylon—a synthetic material capable of being made into a variety of forms including thread and fibers for cloth, known for its toughness, strength and elasticity.

Padding—a layer of resilient material, usually foam, cotton or Dacron, placed next to the cover to provide fullness and the desired firmness.

Panel—any of the several pieces making up the auto interior, most of which are upholstered.

Panel board—composition board, wood paneling or other such material providing a form for upholstering.

Pile—the upright looped or cut fibers on the surface of a fabric; applied especially to carpet, but also referring to cover fabrics.

Pleat—a fold of even width, usually sewn with a hidden seam.

Polypropylene—synthetic fiber better known by brand names such as Herculon and Olefin.

Quarter panel—usually the panel on either side of the vehicle behind the door, or the rear quarter section of the vehicle.

Side panel—any panel covering a side portion of the vehicle interior except a door; also called a quarter panel.

Sinuous spring—seat spring made of heavy-gauge steel wire with zigzag bends, also called zigzag, No-Sag and sagless.

Topstitch—sewing from the top side of the cover material through the padding, resulting in a visible seam.

Tuft—the puffy, raised sections created by drawing down depressions in the surface of an upholstered piece; the process of making tufts.

Tweed—a coarse cloth in a variety of weaves and colors.

Velour—a fabric with a thick, soft nap or pile; the French term for velvet.

Velvet—a fabric with a thick, soft pile or nap.

Vinyl—in upholstery, a material made of a coating of plastic (vinyl) over a knit or woven cloth backing.

Warp—yarns running lengthwise in a woven fabric.

Welt—a cord of fabric used for decoration and to add strength to a seam.

Windlace—a fabric-covered roll forming a seal around door openings.

Woof, weft—filling yarns running across a woven fabric, interlacing the warp yarns.

Sources

Many of the materials and supplies needed for your upholstery job are probably available in your local area. Others, especially specialized items, may be difficult to obtain. Some sources of materials, from accessories to ready-to-install seats and upholstery kits, are listed here.

Unfortunately many wholesale distributors of upholstery materials and supplies deal only with established trim shops. You may do well to develop a relationship with a trimmer in your area through whom you can obtain the materials not available otherwise.

Acme Auto Headlining Company
PO Box 847
Long Beach, CA 90813
    Replacement and custom headliners, windlace, door panel fabric, headliner installation kits

Auto Custom Carpets, Inc.
PO Box 1167
Anniston, AL 36202
    Original-style molded carpet

B-D Company
1361 S. Broadway
Denver, CO 80210
    Carpeting, convertible tops, dyes and vinyl repair kits, upholstering supplies and tools

Ciadella Enterprises, Inc.
3757 E. Broadway, Suite 4
Phoenix, AZ 85040
    Original-style and custom upholstery kits for certain Chevrolet models, 1953 and later, carpets, headliners, convertible tops

Color-Plus
PO Box 404
Kearny, NJ 07032
    Leather and vinyl reconditioning and recoloring products

Hampton Coach
PO Box 665
Hampton, NH 03842
    Original-style upholstery kits for Chevrolet and some Buick models, 1922–54; custom street rod vinyl, velvet, wool and mohair

Hepting Leather Restorations
3469 West 4th Ave.
Denver, CO 80219
    Leather restoration and recoloring

Juliano's Interior Products
321 Talcottville Rd.
Vernon, CT 06066
    Flo-Fit seats, upholstered or unupholstered; fabric, leather, carpet, headliners, upholstery kits, convertible tops, hardware, supplies, sound deadener material

Kanter Auto Products
76 Monroe St.
Boonton, NJ 07005
    Fabric, leather, carpet, upholstery kits, headliners, convertible tops, seat rebuilding kits, supplies

LeBaron Bonney Company
6 Chestnut St.
Amesbury, MA 01913
    Early Ford seats and seat parts, Ford-Mercury upholstery kits, roadster top kits, fabric, leather, carpeting, hardware, tools, supplies

Speedway Motors, Inc.
PO Box 81906
Lincoln, NE 68501
    Fiberglass bucket seats, upholstered and unupholstered

T & R Distributing
PO Box 105
Grand Island, NE 68802
    Portable walking foot industrial sewing machines and sewing machine rental

Tea's Design, Inc.
4909 18th St. SE
Rochester, MN 55904
    Custom seats upholstered in cloth, wool, vinyl or leather; matching upholstery material

Valley Auto Accessories Manufacturing
619 25th Ave.
Rock Island, IL 61201
    Molded door panels, armrest assemblies, seat track adaptor kits

Vintage Friends, Inc.
1218 Carpenter
Humble, TX 77396
    Cerullo seats, upholstered or unupholstered; fabric

L. Walston Auto Interiors
16276 Pine St.
Hesperia, CA 92345
    Original-style seat covers, headliners, carpeting, windlace, fabric

J.C. Whitney & Co.
PO Box 8410
Chicago, IL 60680
    Original-style and custom upholstery kits, carpets, convertible tops, headliners, bucket seats, tools

Index